S0-BEB-166

1001 Ways
to Drive Defensively

1001 Ways to Drive Defensively

HONESTO MARCOS

Copyright © 2014 by Honesto Marcos.

Library of Congress Control Number:		2014900879
ISBN:	Hardcover	978-1-4931-5892-8
	Softcover	978-1-4931-5891-1
	eBook	978-1-4931-5893-5

All rights reserved. No part of this book may be reproduced or transmitted
in any form or by any means, electronic or mechanical, including photocopying,
recording, or by any information storage and retrieval system,
without permission in writing from the copyright owner.

This book was printed in the United States of America.

Rev. date: 04/16/2014

To order additional copies of this book, contact:
Xlibris LLC
1-888-795-4274
www.Xlibris.com
Orders@Xlibris.com
538780

CONTENTS

A. How-To Ideas

B. Principles of Defensive Driving and Accident Avoidance Techniques

Castle Downs Driving School

456-1678

FEES ARE INCOME TAX DEDUCTIBLE

- HELPS TO OBTAIN LEARNER'S PERMIT
- OFFERS COMPETENT INSTRUCTION TO BEGINNERS
- CONDUCTS CLASS 5 EVALUATION
- CLASSROOM INSTRUCTION FOR INSURANCE DISCOUNT
- SPECIALTY: NERVOUS STUDENTS DEFENSIVE
  TECHNIQUES AND PARALLEL PARKING MADE EASY
- PICK-UP AND RETURN SERVICE

12212-144 AVE.

DEDICATION

For inspiring and motivating me while the manuscript was prepared

To

Daughters—Dr. Karen Marcos, Rachelle, and Jessica—their husbands, my nine grandchildren, my wife Aurora, and Mom and Dad, who are now with the Lord.

Police and insurance company that compelled me to take defensive driving and accident avoidance techniques after traffic tickets, where I learned that without knowledge of it, I would be playing with my health and life.

MVO personnel that helped me secure my instructor's and driver's examiner licenses.

Driving instructors that helped me become one of them and school owner for the opportunity to be their instructor till I had my own school.

My students—I owe them for they motivated me to grow with them and gave me the chance to practice the defensive techniques that I am now trying to share.

"Motor vehicle victims, we remember."

Disclaimer

The defensive driving and accident avoidance techniques presented herein have not been evaluated by any governmental body in charge of legislating and promulgating traffic laws and regulations. The ideas, suggestions, and techniques offered here were the products of my many years of driving experience as a driving school operator, driving instructor, and examiner.

I make no warranty, expressed or implied, or assume any legal liability or responsibility for the accuracy, completeness, or usefulness of any information techniques disclosed or represented here that when used will prevent an accident.

Situations, conditions, and skills of the driver, pedestrians' behaviors, and other challenges can't be predicted. Having the knowledge and proper application of defensive driving and accident avoidance techniques can help lessen the severity or even eliminate accidents and thus make driving safer and more enjoyable.

Again, the suggestions and recommendations in this book are guidelines only; the author can't possibly cover all possible driving scenarios, let alone everybody's driving ability. Remember, there are many variables involved whenever we are behind the wheel.

Here are some:

1. The driver's age, physical condition, experience, and emotion.

2. The weather, road condition, local custom, and tradition.

3. The time of the day, volume of traffic, and pedestrians using the road.

4. The type of vehicle or condition of the vehicle one drives.

The defensive driving techniques presented in this book are general guidelines only but should help improve one's driving skill. Make notes, take, and pick what you think will help you improve your ability to apply defensive driving and accident avoidance techniques as you go through this book from cover to cover.

All drivers—young or old, male or female—can benefit from reading and applying the different ideas presented in this book. To instill in everyone the advantages of being a defensive, courteous, and helpful driver, all members of the family should read this book.

This book does not replace your local, provincial, state, or country's operator's manual. The author, the editor, and the publisher advise the reader to check first their driver's manual for comparison and adjustment before one undertakes any of the defensive techniques to conform to local laws and regulations.

To all, have a happy and safe driving.

DRIVER'S BILL OF RIGHTS

1. That every driver has a right to know that he or she has to be physically, mentally, and emotionally fit to drive.

2. That every driver has a right to drive a vehicle suited for the task that is mechanically safe.

3. That every driver has a right to be prepared by knowing ahead the condition of road, weather, and traffic to have a happy and safe driving experience.

4. That every driver has a right to know that without learning defensive driving and accident avoidance techniques, life routines and situations can change, pride can be lost, and/or responsibilities cannot be delivered to loved ones.

5. That every driver has a right to know that defensive driving is like taking life insurance; it serves as protection and an equalizer when confronted by other drivers' mistakes or conditions.

6. That every driver has a right to know that everything good can come to an early end if one is not knowledgeable in defensive driving.

7. That every driver has a right to be helped, given the benefit of the doubt, and not put down regardless of the mistake and who has the right of way.

8.   That every driver has a right not to go through life blaming others but must be prepared and not waste time learning defensive driving that provides the knowledge to help prevent a lifetime of regret.

9.   That every driver has a right to know that even with all the money in the world, if in an accident, whether or not it is his or her fault, one can't buy back the health they used to have.

10.   That every driver has a right to know that a designated driver is a necessity if he is tired, intoxicated, has taken a substance that can impair driving, is sick, and/or is emotionally unstable.

11.   That every driver has a right to know that sooner or later, the delay of learning defensive driving will be paid.

INTRODUCTION

I wrote this book, *1001 Ways to Drive Defensively*, to add knowledge to new or experienced drivers on how to help avoid and prevent accidents, regardless of who is at fault. The techniques were the results of my many years of driving experience, years as a driving instructor, and years as a driver examiner.

Please remember that things never stay the same or are the end of itself. The contents, ideas, defensive techniques might not be applicable in your area. Take and apply what you think will help based on your individual preference.

This book is just to enrich one's knowledge on defensive techniques. I tried to make it as current as much as possible; however, laws and regulations do change. Remember, the only thing constant in life is change. Also, there are numerous variables involved whenever accidents happen. They are the following:

1. Conditions of the two drivers
2. Weather condition
3. Road condition
4. Pedestrians' behavior
5. Type of vehicle involved
6. Local customs and traditions
7. Conditions of the vehicles involved
8. Time of the day it happened
9. Speed of the vehicles involved
10. Driver's knowledge on defensive driving

Although the result can vary when applying defensive driving techniques, it should lessen the severity if involved in a collision. Drivers should not downplay the advantages of knowing defensive driving although not the end in itself as it can be improved.

The defensive techniques are not engraved in stone as health and emotions do change. I can honestly say that the smartest investment one can ever make during their lifetime is having this book to learn more about driving defensively. Why, you ask? Because no amount of money can replace

1. life as a result of a traffic accident or

2. health if injured that impairs, which necessitates a wheelchair for mobility.

Every driver should spend time to read this book, *1001 Ways to Drive Defensively*. Read it frequently to refresh your defensive driving and accident avoidance techniques to

1. enjoy driving more through less stress and avoid road rage;

2. lessen the destruction of property, loss of life, and physical injury; and

3. avoid unnecessary time in court related to traffic.

This book provides knowledge on how to drive defensively in order to be able to help and avoid preventable accidents, no matter who started it. Everyone needs to help and do their part to make the roads safer; no government can do it alone. Let us all combine our talents to find ways to further improve our safety in our ever-expanding number of drivers, vehicles, and road systems.

Drivers who waste their time driving without proper training on defensive driving are playing with his or her life. We can never know too much, nor can we afford to be too macho. Read this book every now and then to remind and refresh our defensive techniques and to continue having a safe and enjoyable driving experience. We have to do our part for the safety of all road users.

The techniques found in this book can be your foundation for safe driving. For as long as we are alive, we depend on motor vehicles for mobility.

The roads are now engineered better, but the sad thing is that statistically, more lives are lost in motor vehicle accidents than in wars. It costs billions of dollars in property damage, and millions of hours are wasted in attending to vehicle accident-related problems.

"Defensive driving is not mandatory but is the best solution
to prevent traffic accidents."

"In driving there are many ways to get into trouble but only one way
to get out of it: by learning and applying defensive driving
and accident avoidance techniques."

MY MISSION STATEMENT

To provide knowledge, ideas, skills, proper attitude, and courtesy in the roads in order to help drivers avoid preventable accidents through defensive driving and accident avoidance techniques regardless of who is at fault or who has the right of way but based on who has the last clear chance to avert a collision. Knowing that in an accident, no amount of wealth can bring back the health or life that one used to have. Especially, it takes only a second or two to avoid a lifetime of regret.

Notice to All Readers

To the millions of readers, supporters, and contributors of this book, *1001 Ways to Drive Defensively*, let me express my deepest appreciation and thank you for your interest, encouragement, and recommendation that will undoubtedly be for the benefit of all road users that will read this book and apply the techniques mentioned herein.

Of course, the author welcomes everyone's feedback and encourages you to send your driving experiences with the public or the police that are funny, memorable, strange, or educational. Also include anecdotes and jokes.

You can mail them to

PO Box 73054 Las Vegas NV 89170-3054.

We will try to include them in the next issue with your name or, if you prefer, your pen name.

So in the name of safety for all, any ideas, articles, and suggestions you could recommend or contribute to benefit us all will be very much appreciated, because we are all in this crusade.

All contributions will motivate and inspire us to make and adjust the succeeding edition for the public's reading pleasure.

Be an agent of change and be a part of the solution.

Our crusade is to make the roads safer and a relaxing place to drive by lessening the loss of life and the destruction of properties due to traffic-related accidents.

Again from me to all of you—a million thanks.

A. HOW-TO IDEAS

CHAPTER 1

Advantages of Wearing Seat Belts and Having Air Bags

Both were designed

1. to cushion vehicle occupants from potential life-threatening and debilitating injury if there's an accident by reducing the impact regardless of who is at fault;

2. to prevent vehicle occupants from moving forward and hitting the steering wheel, dashboard, and/or windshield that can injure the head, chest, and neck, causing whiplash;

3. to help save the government from spending medical-related expenses, reduce insurance premiums, and avoid traffic tickets in case of an accident; and

4. to save lives and prevent vehicle occupants from being sentenced to a wheelchair and prevent the loss of life and/or health.

Note

a. To protect the vehicle occupants, both the lap and shoulder belts work as a system. Without the other, it is not as effective. They have to be properly restrained or positioned. But remember, they never prevent accidents; they only lessen the gravity.

Chapter 2

Deadliest Collision Is Between Motor Vehicle and Train

1. I must be cautious as I approach a railroad crossing. I listen for an approaching train and check visually from left to right. Even if there is no stop sign or signal, I should be ready to stop, no closer than five meters from the nearest rail.

2. If I'm in doubt of my safety because it is not that easy to accurately judge a train's speed, I must not attempt to cross.

3. I must check before I move forward after the last car of the train that just passed. A second train can come from another track from the opposite direction.

4. I don't change gears while crossing the tracks with a standard vehicle to avoid possible stalling and getting stuck right on the rail.

5. I must get everyone out of my vehicle if I stall on the rail crossing and move all far from the tracks so that nobody gets hit by flying debris.

6. I must never try to beat the train no matter how much in a hurry I am, because it will not give me a second chance. A train can't stop in time to miss a vehicle.

7. If a gate is down, I can't proceed around it even if there's no train coming or visible.

8. I must stop at all railroad crossings if I drive a school or passenger bus or truck or if my load is flammable or are dangerous materials.

9. I must never follow a vehicle ahead until I have space to clear the rails so as not to block, occupy, or stop on the rail if the vehicle I am following stops.

Note

a. Safety should take precedence over hurry.

b. Defensive driving is first in safety.

CHAPTER 3

Drowsy Driver is Dangerous Behind the Wheel

1. An impaired and tired driver are both dangerous; they have slow reaction time and are less alert.

2. According to research, drivers that are drowsy can fall asleep without actually being aware.

3. Drowsy drivers can be dangerous to others or to themselves if they have not slept or haven't had enough sleep.

4. Drowsy drivers must not get behind the wheel if they did not have adequate sleep or rest. Safety should take precedence over hurry.

5. Drowsy drivers should not depend on coffee to overcome the effect of drowsiness while driving; no scientific evidence has proven this to be.

6. Drowsy drivers driving alone are inviting trouble. Have somebody to talk with and to alert you of possible danger or to take over the driving.

Warning Signs of a Drowsy Driver

1. Tilting head forward unintentionally, frequently yawning, has difficulty keeping his/her eyes open, and focusing on traffic and traffic signs.

2. Has difficulty concentrating on the driving task, mind is wandering, late in recognizing pedestrian's situation.

3. Has a hard time keeping his/her lane, tailgating, has near-crashes, and keeps hitting the buttons separating the lanes and rumble strips on the edge of the road.

Note

a. Drowsy drivers had caused collisions and run off the road, resulting in injury or even death.

CHAPTER 4

Due to Motorcycle's Limitations and Quick Acceleration

1. Cyclists should always remember that

    a. a motorcycle has only two wheels and is thus less stable;

    b. it accelerates quickly, making it less visible and hard to anticipate;

    c. the rider has no protection like a seat belt, air bag, and no protective shell like a car;

    d. it slides easily with strong wind and on rough, muddy, or wet roads due to light weight; and

    e. vehicles that stop behind to give plenty of space, more if road is slippery and when it's dark.

2. If I ride a motorcycle, I must do the following:

    a. Maintain posted speed limit and adjust speed according to road or weather condition. Safety takes precedence over hurry.

    b. Stay out of blind spots of other drivers as I have to be seen. I wear protective body gear and an approved helmet, knowing that my head is vulnerable in a crash.

c.   Make eye contact with the other driver and double-check before any maneuver. Check all intersections regardless of who has the right of way, and use no alcohol or drug.

d.   For better understanding on road safety, read on defensive driving and accident avoidance techniques, because sooner or later, the delay will be paid.

e.   Understand that no one can predict when an accident will occur, but with defensive driving, one is ready when it comes.

Note

a.   Vehicles that stop behind a motorcycle should give plenty of space, especially if the road is slippery and when dark.

b.   Everyone has one life and good health. Don't be an organ donor by being irresponsible.

CHAPTER 5

Effects of Driving Under the Influence

It changes the way a person thinks and acts. It interferes by affecting one's judgment and coordination. It can be

1. due to alcohol only, prescribed drug, or a combination of both;

2. due to depressants, stimulants, narcotics, or hallucinogens; or

3. due to other mind-altering drug that works as a sedative, which

    A. affects judgment and coordination and slows reaction time;

    B. makes a person drowsy, confused, and emotionally unstable; and

    C. can potentially increase the chance of being in a crash.

4. The following could be controlled, prescribed drugs, or over-the-counter medications:

    a. Marijuana

    b. Tranquilizers

    c. Cold medicines

    d. Cocaine

e.   Sleeping pills

f.   Allergy medicines

5.   And the results if charged are the following:

a.   Loss of self-esteem

b.   Loss of reputation

c.   Feeling of guilt

d.   Loss of wage

e.   Loss or suspension of license

f.   Financially expensive

g.   Criminal penalties may be imposed

h.   Increase of insurance premiums

i.   Fees for towing and impounding

j.   Jail sentence

K.   Attend DUI School

l.   Suspension of vehicle registration

6.   Who are those considered drinking drivers?

a.   The social drinkers—they show no sign of being under the influence of alcohol.

b.   The ones who do not seem obviously drunk. They can manage to even walk straight.

c.   Those who talk intelligently and coherently and give the appearance of sobriety although intoxicated.

    d.   Research shows that the judgment and ability to react quickly to avoid accidents are impaired, including the ones that think a few drinks will not affect their ability to drive.

7.   Effect of Alcohol

    a.   The major cause of serious vehicular accidents.

    b.   It usually happens during holiday season, like Christmas, or whenever there's celebration.

8.   One does not have to be obviously drunk but can still be under the influence of alcohol if one

    a.   loses some clearness of mind and self-control;

    b.   believes that a few drinks will not affect their driving ability; or

    c.   shows slow judgment, reaction, reflex, and ability to act quickly for safety.

9.   The things to consider when it comes to consumption of alcohol are the following:

    a.   One's gender, body weight, and the type of alcohol that one is consuming

    b.   Amount, kind of food consumed, emotional condition, and/or fatigue of the driver

    c.   Social or occasional drinker, full or empty stomach

    d.   The speed of consumption of liquor

    e.   The mixture of different types of alcohol and type of mix used

    f.   Coffee will not overcome the effect of alcohol or other stimulants

    g.   The alcohol content in the bloodstream depends on the amount of alcohol consumed, and the time to elapse plays a role.

10. Some clues that a driver is under the influence and/or impaired

   a. Turning wide and erratic speed

   b. Narrowly hitting other vehicles

   c. Following too close

   d. Braking erratically

   e. Driving in wrong lane

   f. Straddling lanes

   g. Driving too slowly for condition of the road

   h. Stopping for no reason

   i. Being slow in responding to traffic signals

   j. Driving without headlight on at night

Note

If I have consumed alcohol, I

   a. get somebody to do the driving, or I take the taxi or bus—it is cheaper than a fine and less hassle; and

   b. have to know that a full stomach tends to slow the rate of alcohol absorption to the bloodstream, especially with oily food.

CHAPTER 6

How Can I Avoid Hitting Wild Animals?

1. When I drive in the country or forested and/or mountainous areas, I scan for animals well ahead.

2. I have to be extra careful at dusk and dawn as they tend to move around to feed at this time.

3. I slow down and look around in areas where there are animal-crossing signs posted.

4. If I see one animal, there may be more as wild animals move in herds.

5. If an animal suddenly appears in front of me,

    a. I decide quickly if I can stop safely.

    b. If not, I need to figure out if I can steer around the animal.

    c. If so, I leave lots of room around the animal as a frightened animal may run in any direction.

    d. If I choose to steer into the path of opposite traffic, I must be sure that it is clear as head-on collision is deadly.

    e. If the ditch is not that deep, it might be a better choice to ditch my vehicle rather than run into a head-on collision or hit the animal directly.

f.   Hitting the animal directly, it can get inside the vehicle through the windshield.

g.   A wounded and scared animal inside a vehicle can become very aggressive and can hurt the occupants.

Note

a.   Defensive driving is the difference that makes safe driving possible.

b.   Safety belongs to those who learn defensive driving.

CHAPTER 7

How Can I Identify a Drunk Driver?

1. They straddle lanes, use two lanes, and/or follow too close.

2. They make turns too wide, cut corners, weave, and/or drift from lane to lane.

3. They almost hit another vehicle or road signs and stop in traffic for no obvious reason.

4. They drive too slow for the posted speed limit or road condition, and speed is not smooth.

5. They turn abruptly to the wrong lane and swerve to correct position.

6. They don't turn on headlights at night, don't signal to indicate intentions, or forget to cancel.

7. They drift into other lanes and don't anticipate or respond properly to traffic signs.

8. They use their brake erratically in an uneven, jerky way and/or ride on their brake.

Note

a. To prevent accidents and the increase of insurance fees, I report to the police any suspected drunk driver.

CHAPTER 8

How Can I Improve Gas Mileage in Relation to My Vehicle?

1. Having a hybrid vehicle with five manual transmission, cruise control, and overdrive, with engine and the type of vehicle suited for my need.

2. Having a locking gas cap tightly closed to reduce evaporation, prevent thieves, and avoid seeing the "check engine" sign on the instrument panel.

3. Removing nonessential stuff from my vehicle's trunk and roof rack—they cause drag.

4. Having quality tires properly inflated for safety and balanced and aligned to reduce wear and tear.

5. Using the recommended grade of motor oil for different seasons, preferably synthetic oil for better quality and longer time between oil changes.

6. Replacing the air filter every oil change or sooner if clogged and regularly checking all fluid levels.

7. Consulting the owner's manual as to recommended octane level. Filling up gas at night when cooler and in the middle of the week—it is usually cheaper than weekends.

8. Having regular tune-up and emission control checked by a qualified mechanic.

9. Closing my sunroof and windows especially at highways where speed is fast.

10. Trading my old vehicle for a brand-new or slightly used certified vehicle.

11. Minimizing the use of the air-conditioning during summer.

12. Making sure not to fill my gas tank to the top, especially on hot days, due to evaporation.

CHAPTER 9

How Can I Lane Change or Pass a Vehicle Safely?

1. I scan well ahead for hazards—if clear, I check my inside and outside mirror, then my blind spot to check the space gap for traffic behind to know if I can change lanes safely.

2. If everything is okay, I signal my intention, warn the driver ahead, and then check the outside mirror again.

3. When clear, I make a gradual lane change, obtain a speed advantage, and then recheck the condition ahead.

4. Create return space, check right-side blind spot, and then signal right.

5. When I see the whole front of the vehicle I have just passed, I change lanes while still checking my inside mirror to make sure our distance is appropriate.

CHAPTER 10

How I Avoid Head-On Collision

I do any of the following:

1. I select one that is less damaging either by stopping or speeding and steering my vehicle toward anything that is soft like a snowbank or bushes instead of a big tree or light post.

2. I steer toward a vehicle instead of hitting a pedestrian, a cyclist, or a motorized wheelchair—not hitting directly any stationary, immovable, and/or heavy objects, but sideswiping it only to soften the impact.

3. I steer toward traffic that is moving in the same direction or steer straight to a ditch that is not that deep rather than into a head-on collision with oncoming traffic.

Note

a. I must be alert to know situations that might develop into problems by reading the road condition well ahead.

b. I have to read and learn defensive driving and accident avoidance techniques to know quickly the defense of any traffic challenges

c. To predict the future, I create it.

CHAPTER 11

How I Check Intersections with Traffic Lights

I do the following:

1. If I stop for a red light, before I proceed forward on green, I quickly check traffic from left to right. Somebody might be racing the red lights, or there could be an emergency vehicle approaching nearby. If I count by saying "thousand and one, thousand and two" only before I proceed forward, without visually checking traffic from left to right is not a safe procedure.

2. As I approach green traffic lights, I scan the intersection left and right to make sure I know if it is safe to proceed. Even though I have the right of way, it will not prevent me from going to where I don't plan to go yet if somebody makes a mistake and runs a red light.

3. When I am about a block away from an intersection with green lights, if I see a "walk" sign, I know the light is new, but if I have the "don't walk" sign or stale green, it means the lights are about to turn yellow. I cover my brake, check traffic condition behind, and if somebody is following too close, I tap my brake to warn them that I might stop.

4. If I don't check early whether I have a stale green or not, I will not know what to expect well in advance. I will run either a yellow light or a red light, which is against traffic regulations. Worse, I can be in an accident, get physically hurt, or end my life, get a traffic ticket, increase insurance premiums, or incur financial loss and/or personal liability.

CHAPTER 12

How I Check My Brake After Driving through Water

1. Soon after going through deep water, my brake could be affected; either it loses the holding power or the vehicle pulls in one side when brakes are applied.

2. This happens after going through rain, or worse, if muddy, the brakes can be very slippery, thus losing its grip on the vehicle.

3. Also, it could make the vehicle pull in one side because the brakes are not working evenly as some pads are more slippery than the others.

4. Until my brakes work normally by stopping my vehicle properly, I test my brakes by applying light pressure intermittently on low gear and slow speed without delay after going through water.

Note

    a. As a defensive driver, when I go through deep or not-so-deep water, it is better to be sure that the vehicle's braking power is not lost, especially with water that is oily or muddy and is slippery.

    b. I don't endanger my family and self for something I can do easily for safety.

CHAPTER 13

How I Drive Defensively on Ice or Snow

1. I adjust my driving to conform to the weather and road conditions, regardless of posted speed limit.

2. I have to be aware that bridges and overpasses tend to freeze first.

3. I avoid a sudden start, stop, or change of speed and direction.

4. I always keep my windows clear of snow or fog.

5. I use my lower gear when negotiating thick snow.

6. When approaching red light, I adjust my speed; hopefully, I will not stop before the green light.

7. To avoid stopping abruptly and risk being rear-ended, I adjust my speed on stale-green lights, check traffic behind, and cover and tap my brake to warn traffic if close behind.

8. I slow down early at stop signs and red lights commensurate to the weather, road condition, and traffic behind.

9. I must always brake cautiously, never abruptly, because it can cause my vehicle to slide, spin around, or cause an accident by going to the wrong lane, to the ditch, or to hit another vehicle.

10. I never gun my vehicle when starting from slippery surfaces; it will only cause the tires to spin. Instead, I release the brake, let the vehicle move on its own, and then slowly press the accelerator pedal after the vehicle has gained momentum.

Chapter 14

How I Drive if I Have a Front-Tire Blowout

1. When my front tire suddenly loses air, without panic, I hold the steering wheel firmly in a straight direction as my vehicle will pull to the side of the blowout.

2. I ease my pressure off the accelerator pedal and don't apply my brake so that my vehicle will not skid.

3. Then I check traffic opening for a lane change; if favorable, I signal my intention to move off the road while I continue checking traffic behind.

4. Once I have slowed down and I'm in control of my vehicle, I gently apply my brakes to stop and steer away from the traveled portion of the road.

5. For a back-tire blowout, I do the same procedure as above, but it is much easier to handle and execute than a front-tire blowout.

Note

a. If I have to stop on the side of the road for any reason, knowing that it's very dangerous, I make sure I park way off the roadway with my flashers on and my early warning device properly positioned. While the repair is being done or while waiting for help, I also make sure nobody is left inside the vehicle.

b.   Especially at night when it is foggy, raining, and/or snowing and visibility is poor, drivers can get easily confused and think a parked vehicle ahead is moving and crash into it.

CHAPTER 15

How I Drive Safely in the Rain

1. I start to drive slowly to get the feel of the road and activate my windshield wipers with a speed commensurate to the volume of raindrops falling.

2. To have good visibility and to avoid the windshield from fogging, I put my defroster on, use a low-beam headlight, and watch for the slow-moving vehicles ahead.

3. I keep my speed well below dry pavement, based on the condition of the road surface and since visibility is usually poor.

4. Due to tires having less contact with the road, which also increases stopping distance, for my safety, I allow myself extra time to get to my destination knowing that water makes the road slippery.

5. I apply my brakes early and gently and increase my following distance so I can stop safely and avoid skidding.

6. I constantly check my inside and outside rearview mirrors for traffic behind and the intersections for signs and traffic, to prepare early for the appropriate speed and what to do.

7. I test my brake every time I pass a flooded area to make sure it is working as it should. I look down ahead if visibility is poor and use the road markings to help guide me to my lane.

8.   I have to be gentle on my steering as it is more sensitive due to the road being wet, and reduce my speed on curves.

Note

a.   I should not stop on the traveled portion of the road if I have to stop.

b.   I have to make sure my tires have deep tread, have plenty of washer fluid, and that the windshield wipers and defroster are in good working condition.

CHAPTER 16

How I Drive Safely When I'm Near Trucks, Especially Tractor Trailers

Because they are larger and heavier than my car, they usually win if I'm in a collision with them. My vehicle gets demolished; my passengers and I, the driver, will all get injured or even killed. So I do the following:

1. On gravel or muddy roads, I double my following distance behind a truck, especially when raining or in wintertime. They spray muddy water, rocks, and other debris. This also happens when I'm being passed; I activate my windshield even before they approach me. For this reason, my windshield reservoir should always be full.

2. Due to their size, normally, they have a wider blind spot. I must see the truck driver's face through their outside rearview mirror; this makes them see me and know of my presence.

3. I never stop my vehicle close to the truck when they stop on a hill; sometimes they roll back when they start due to gravity or when they engage their clutch to shift gears.

4. When nearing intersections with red lights or stop signs, I don't change lanes to the lane in front of the truck. Due to their size, they will not be able to stop before colliding into my vehicle. The driver will not expect or be ready for my sudden move.

5.   Of course I don't attempt to pass trucks on two-lane roads, near the top of a hill, winding or coming to a curve, if I have a solid yellow line on my side, and where I don't see far enough ahead to make sure I will be safe. Due to the truck size, I will need more time to pass.

6.   I have to see the whole front of the truck from my inside rearview mirror before I pull back into my lane, the same principle I use in other passing maneuver.

7.   When a tractor trailer turns left or right, even if I see a big space next to the truck enough to squeeze my vehicle, I won't attempt; this is very dangerous. If I do, I will be flattened as the space is needed when the trailer and tractor straightens itself.

CHAPTER 17

How I Jump-Start My Vehicle

1. Both vehicles should be close to each other but not touching, with gears in park; all accessories off; if manual transmission, I have it on neutral; and both ignitions off.

2. I attach the positive red jumper cable to the positive (+) terminal of the booster or good battery.

3. Then I attach the other end of the positive red cable to the positive (+) terminal of the dead or discharged battery.

4. Next I attach one end of the negative black jumper cable to the negative (−) terminal of the good or booster battery.

5. Then I attach the other end of the black cable to the negative (−) terminal of the dead or discharged battery or to the unpainted metal of the engine of the disabled vehicle.

6. Next I start the jumper vehicle and run the engine fast for a couple of minutes to let the dead battery gain some charge. Then I start the disabled vehicle; if it does not start, I check the connections for tightness.

7. Once the disabled vehicle starts, I remove the jumper cables by reversing the sequence. First, I disconnect the negative (−) black cable from the engine or from the negative (−) terminal of the dead battery, then I disconnect the other end from the booster battery.

8. Then I disconnect the positive (+) cable from the dead battery or disabled vehicle; finally, I disconnect the other end from the booster battery.

Note

    a.   I make sure that I wear eye protection before I start connecting or removing the jumper cables.

    b.   So as not to damage the electrical components of the vehicles, I make sure the cable ends don't touch each other.

CHAPTER 18

How I Rock Out My Vehicle from Snow

1. First, I move forward in low gear, accelerating slowly; too much gas makes the wheels spin.

2. Then I shift quickly to reverse and back up slowly until my wheels start to spin.

3. Next, I shift back to low gear, changing direction forward quickly and rocking the vehicle.

4. Until I have enough clear runway to build speed, I repeat this movement in rapid succession.

Note

    a. To rock a vehicle from snow, it needs practice and lots of patience.

    b. Shovel snow off and place a piece of rug or sand in the front and back of tires for better traction.

CHAPTER 19

How My Driving Habits Help Save Gas

1. By choosing the best route based on traffic volume, number of traffic lights, and time of the day before I get behind the wheel. My destinations that are close to each other—I study, analyze, arrange, and combine them.

2. By accelerating, changing lanes smoothly, maintaining steady speed, and coasting whenever possible, like when approaching a red light or stop sign. Thus, I need to anticipate traffic signs and conditions by checking well ahead of my lane to adjust speed, to remain in motion, and to stop smoothly if needed.

3. By relaxing when behind a convoy of vehicles or a procession, keeping my vehicle moving by coordinating the pressure I apply on my gas pedal and the brake and not losing the momentum that was built.

4. By refraining from using the brake too often, no tailgating, no panic stopping, and anticipating traffic conditions well ahead so as not to waste gas and shorten the life of the brake mechanism.

5. By driving on the freeways as much as possible and not going over the posted speed limit. I use the overdrive gear if available and activate the cruise control when traffic permits. I close the windows to reduce drag and remove excess weights from the trunk.

6. By avoiding unnecessary idling for a long period in winter, only thirty seconds is needed to circulate engine oil. Before I drive slowly, I make sure that the windshield is clear and not fogged up.

7. By installing a block heater, timed to come on two hours before I plan to drive, to warm engine during winter. In warm weather, a shady place, a carport, or a garage is the best place to park so as to minimize using of air condition.

8. By letting my fingers do the walking, double-checking addresses on appointments, having GPS to locate addresses easily, shopping through the World Wide Web, and having grocery delivered. I avoid going to drive-through fast-food restaurants; too much time is wasted waiting for the order.

9. By always double-checking parking brake before starting, increasing speed before climbing a hill, using the appropriate gear for going up or down, and adjusting speed according to conditions ahead.

10. By taking roads that are less congested and with less traffic lights. I take the freeway if available, carpool with coworkers, or take public transportation. For short distances, I walk or cycle.

11. By observing traffic conditions well ahead to know if somebody is turning, changing lanes, or doing anything that can cause traffic conflict. I ease up on my gas pedal; I might need to help, and so I don't have to brake hard. Also, on red lights, stop signs, or yield signs, I time my arrival by easing on my accelerator pedal, but my speed will be based on the traffic condition behind me.

12. By not using gas-saving gadgets—they can damage my car's engine; can't achieve the savings they claim. I have a mechanic check if I'm buying a used vehicle. Be wary about the words *as is*, which mean "no warranty." In areas that have winter, a front-wheel vehicle is preferable; it does not spin as much on slippery surfaces or get stuck easily.

13. By filling up in the morning and using recommended gas grade. I don't overfill the tank; gas level should not be below half before filling up. Dirt that settled at the bottom can clog the gas line. I use the proper gas cup and make sure the radiator cap is working properly to maintain the proper temperature of the engine.

CHAPTER 20

More Ways to Save on Gas

1. Buy a hybrid vehicle.

2. Buy a locking gas cap to prevent thieves.

3. No drive-through fast-food restaurants—too much time wasted waiting for the order.

4. Remove roof racks if not needed; they cause drag.

5. Close sunroof at highways and when traveling fast.

6. Buy quality and properly inflated tires for safety.

7. Always have wheels aligned and balanced.

8. Use synthetic oil—the best quality—it gives longer time between oil changes.

9. Check all fluid levels and air filters regularly.

10. Have emission control checked regularly by a qualified mechanic.

11. Fill up gas at night, at midweek, or before going for a holiday.

12. Tighten gas cap to reduce vaporization, damage to the emission control system, fuel economy and to avoid seeing "check engine" sign on the instrument panel.

13. Park in a shady place if at all possible.

14. Buy a manual five-speed transmission, if practical.

15. Get rid of unnecessary items from the vehicle or trunk.

16. Buy a brand-new or slightly used vehicle instead of an old one, if one can afford.

17. Let the fingers do the walking through telephone, texting, and Internet.

18. Do not own a vehicle to save gas, other expenses, and hassles of owning one.

19. Take the taxi occasionally, have grocery delivered, and dwell close to amenities.

CHAPTER 21

Reasons Why I Check Every Intersection

At every intersection, I have to be aware of the signs from each direction. Since intersections are where most accidents do happen, I never refuse to help if needed. This includes parking lots' entrances, exits, back alleys, and wherever traffic or pedestrians can cross each other's paths.

Even though I have the right of way, I still check every intersection to make sure I am safe. I don't leave my safety to anyone. I check from left to right at least twice, depending on how busy the road is.

Why Do I Bother Checking Intersections and Helping When It Is My Right of Way?

The reason is, although it is my right of way, if there is an accident, and even if it is not my fault, it will not prevent me from getting hurt. So I help and apply defensive driving techniques for my safety. No doubt most drivers will observe and follow the road signs, but some will not always yield or stop to give me my right of way. So why will I take chances and let somebody decide the state of my health and future if all I need is only a second to help and prevent it?

It is common knowledge that better-built vehicles, roads, highways, and byways make driving easier for everyone but have not lowered the loss of life, physical injury, and/or property damage; instead, they have even increased. Need is the mother of invention, so defensive driving and accident avoidance techniques were born.

As long as human beings are involved, there will always be challenges that no amount of money and engineering can solve or eliminate completely, thus the need to be a defensive driver as an equalizer for any challenges that drivers might encounter in the road, like the following:

1. Situations originated by nature or man-made—some drivers won't know what to do

2. Drivers that are irresponsible and inconsiderate or refuse to help

3. Drivers that have physical challenges due to age or vice

4. Impaired drivers due to alcohol and other mind-altering substances

5. Tired and sleepy due to a prescribed drug

6. Worried about work-related problems

7. Drowsy due to shift work or too long at the wheel

8. Having an epileptic seizure or suicidal

9. Having a financial problem and worried about it

10. Experiencing marital problems and thinking about it

11. In a hurry and not concerned about safe driving

12. Overjoyed after receiving good news

13. Depressed after receiving negative news

14. Not aware of police vehicle presence on an emergency call

15. Not aware of an ambulance on an emergency call

16. Not aware of a fire truck on an emergency call

17. From out of town, not familiar with the area

18. Not aware of pedestrians that are jaywalking or hidden

19. Not aware of elderly pedestrian or pedestrian with physical challenges

20. Daydreaming, not concentrating on the driving task

21. Texting or talking on their cell phones

22. Blinded by the sun and/or reflection from a building

23. Experiencing poor visibility due to snow, rain, and/or fog

24. Experiencing a hypoglycemic or hyperglycemic reaction

25. Having a stroke or a heart attack

26. Being chased by police, won't care about safety

27. Speeding or racing with somebody

28. Speeding after robbing a bank

29. Driving a vehicle with a mechanical problem

30. Following too close and/or applying the brake too late

31. Experiencing a traction problem due to snow or rain

32. Obstructed by bushes, vehicles, or commercial signs

33. Distracted by loud music and/or noisy passengers

34. Worried about divorce or other legal problems

35. Worried about money loss in gambling or business

36. Not checking or following traffic rules and regulations

Knowing that drivers sometimes fail to follow road signs and traffic regulations, I cannot be too complacent even if it is my right of way. I have to be a defensive driver, knowing that intersections are where traffic meets from different directions and so where an accident mostly happens. If I am in an accident, I have only myself to blame if I get hurt or wreck my vehicle.

I will not trade my life or health for something I can easily prevent. As part of being defensive, I have to be always

1. courteous, helpful, and forgiving to every driver and/or any road user and ready to apply defensive driving and accident avoidance techniques when needed.

Drivers are judged by their ability to avoid an accident regardless of who has the right of way. As a defensive driver, I have to help eliminate or lessen the danger of any driving situation that comes my way, because if an accident happens, it will not

1. make me feel better if I get hurt, especially if I could have easily prevented it;

2. prevent me from spending money to fight my case and wasting time in court;

3. prevent me from paying higher insurance premiums and affecting my credit ratings;

4. help me to fulfill my goals and ambitions in life if my health is impaired;

5. help me continue my profession or hobby if my physical condition is below par;

6. help me continue my support to the dreams and ambitions of loved ones; and

7. prevent me from going six feet below the ground or, worse, dead but buried a few years later.

I know and believe that most, if not all, accidents are preventable if only we do our part by being an agent of change. Without learning defensive driving, it will not be sufficient to make one a safe driver even if one passes the driving road test. Learning the principles and knowing how to apply defensive driving and accident avoidance techniques are necessary especially if one was taught by a relative or friend or was self-taught. To be a defensive driver, I have to know what to do:

a.   If it's raining, to avoid hydroplaning, and the proper speed for road conditions

b.   If there's a bright sun in the early morning or late afternoon, glaring on my eyes

c.   If it's wintertime, how to prepare my vehicle, myself, what to carry, and the challenges

d.   If I drive at night, when it is foggy or windy, or when there's a flash flood

Note

a.   I can't be a Monday-morning quarterback saying, "I should have . . . it's too late." I have to be prepared and ready for any possible adversity, right then and there.

b.   Every good man or woman doing nothing to improve the safety in the road to better protect himself or herself, his or her family, and others is a disservice to humanity. Every driver out there is our brother or sister from a different mother or is a friend we have not met.

CHAPTER 22

Safety Procedures I Follow When Fueling

1. I never smoke or light matches or a lighter nearby.

2. I turn my vehicle ignition off before fueling.

3. I do not overfill my gas tank, and I inform the attendant if there's a spill.

4. I do not use my cell phone while fueling; it can start a fire.

5. I hold the nozzle handle to prevent it from slipping off the tank while fueling.

6. To avoid static electricity, I touch a metal or the gas nozzle before I open the gas tank.

7. Fire can start as I touch the gas nozzle, due to static electricity, if I go back inside the vehicle.

8. I do not pull the gas nozzle out if fire does occur as a result of static electricity, because it will spread more gas, causing a bigger fire.

Note

    a. If I drive a recreational vehicle that has cooking or heating appliances, their pilot should be off before fueling is started.

    b. I fill no more than one container at a time, and the container is grounded.

CHAPTER 23

Steps I Do to Pass Safely

1.   I do not just pass a vehicle or bus that has stopped or slowed down. Instead I prepare for the possibility to stop in case a pedestrian, bicycle, or power scooter is at the same time wanting to cross my path but is hidden from my view.

2.   When I see such a situation, I right away check my rearview mirror to find out the traffic situation behind me. If vehicles are following too close, I tap my brake, slow down to avoid being rear-ended, and cover my brake, ready to stop if I have to, as I check down the front of the stopped vehicle for anybody that might cross my path.

3.   To help my fellow drivers, if I'm ahead and I see a pedestrian wanting to cross the street with no pedestrian crosswalk, I right away check the traffic behind. If there's traffic close behind me, I discourage the people from crossing by not stopping but keep moving slowly and be ready to stop. If they insist on crossing, I give a hand signal to the traffic behind to stop.

4.   City buses are the most dangerous to pass. They drop or pick up passengers, and for whatever reason, sometimes people don't check properly before they cross the road. It's true—they have the right of way, but who gets hurt or killed? As a responsible and defensive driver, if my view is obstructed, it is up to me, for everybody's safety, to prepare for and expect the worst. If possible, I make a lane change to leave one lane between me and the bus for space caution but still be ready to stop if needed.

5. I must not pass if a driver is looking at a street sign even if they're holding me up, not until I know which way they are going. Also, I don't pass if a driver had slowed down or stopped for no visible reason; it could be because a pedestrian is hidden and crossing.

6. I don't attempt to pass if I'm near an intersection or railroad crossing or if there's a long line of vehicles ahead. However, if somebody is suicidal and tries to pass regardless of the situation, I help by creating a space for them to squeeze in ahead of me.

Chapter 24

Things That Can Affect My Safety When I Pass in the Highway

I don't attempt in the following situations:

1. If I'm on a hill, approaching blind curves, and there's immediate oncoming traffic.

2. If I'm close to bridges, abutments, and railroad crossings.

3. If another driver is holding me back and if my sight distance is limited.

4. If there is a double solid line or where there are signs prohibiting it.

5. If there's another vehicle from behind me that is also signaling to pass.

6. If a driver slows down or signals to turn; they could be confused of what to do.

7. If an oncoming vehicle is too close ahead on a two-lane roadway.

8. If the maneuver cannot be completed before reaching a "no-passing zone" sign.

9. If a vehicle ahead is at or near speed limit.

10. If the vehicle I am passing speeds up, I have to abort the lane change.

Note

When I Am Being Passed

a. Whether I agree or not, instead of trying to compete with the driver, I find it safer to allow them to pass me, because by giving a second or two, I will gain the benefit of not being in an accident.

b. It is not only dangerous but also shows no manners and courtesy on my part if I speed up when somebody is trying to pass me.

c. I also move a little to the right and slow down so the passing vehicle can get in front of my vehicle much easier and faster.

CHAPTER 25

What Can Compromise My Safety When I Drive at Night

1. Not aligned headlights, defective or dirty taillights, signal lights, and windshield.

2. Poor eyesight, empty windshield reservoir, wipers that are not working properly.

3. If I overdrive my headlights by driving faster and farther than what my headlights can illuminate.

4. The glare will bother my eyes if I look directly at the bright lights of the oncoming traffic; instead, I look down at the road edge or the center line.

Note:

a. There are more traffic accidents happening at night due to limited vision, so I make frequent stops to stretch and relax for fresh air and a light snack.

b. I only use my high beam in open country and use my low beam when following or when there's oncoming traffic.

c. When it is rainy, snowing, foggy, and cloudy, for better visibility and safety, I have my lights on, day or night, and on low beam.

CHAPTER 26

What Can I Do if My Brake Fails?

1. I pump the brakes several times, but I do not pump a vehicle equipped with antilock brakes.

2. If still not working, I apply the emergency parking brake gradually but hold the release button firmly and release it slightly when I sense my vehicle is going to skid.

3. If my engine stalls or stops and my vehicle is equipped with power brake, I still have brake, but have to push the pedal hard with steady pressure.

4. If the wheels lock, I ease up on the brake pedal and then apply the brake again but with much lighter pressure.

5. I sideswipe something to slow down my vehicle, or if available, I steer into an emergency runway if the vehicle is still out of control.

6. In order to pull over to the side of the road, I check for an opening, sound my horn, and activate my four-way flasher if the vehicle starts to be under control.

I have a mechanic check my brake system without delay if

1. there's a scraping or grinding noise coming from the brakes;

2. when I apply the brake, it feels spongy or soft and my vehicle pulls to the side; and

3. when the brake system warning light stays illuminated in the instrument panel.

Note

a. I use the low gear to prevent wear and overheating my brakes when I'm going downhill for long stretches. I never shift to neutral.

b. I do not believe I save gas using neutral going downhill; the truth is, I save my life and my passengers!

c. I regularly check my brake fluid level.

CHAPTER 27

What Can I Do if My Vehicle Overheats?

1. While driving, I keep glancing at the temperature gauge to see if the needle is at normal range.

2. I activate my heater at high speed to get more air through the radiator if the temperature is higher than normal, and I turn off my air condition.

3. If still high, I check for a safe place to pull over, way off the traveled portion of the road, and let the engine idle for a few minutes to see if the pointer drops back to normal range.

4. If temperature remains high, I turn the engine off then carefully open the hood to help cool down the engine before I check for possible problems, like the following:

    a. Leaking hose—I seal it with tapes, if available.

    b. Plastic coolant container—I add water or antifreeze, if empty.

    c. Fan belts—if loose, I tighten if tools are available.

    d. Engine oil—I check for fluid level and add oil if available.

5. If overheating remains and is beyond my ability to fix, I call for service.

6. Possible Reasons for Engine to Overheat

a. Low coolant level

b. Sticking thermostat

c. Low on engine oil

d. Hot weather

e. Towing a trailer

f. Clogged radiator or heater core

g. Loose or broken engine-drive belt

h. Damaged radiator hose

i. Going up on mountain grades

j. Stop-and-go traffic

Note

a. I never open the radiator cap when the engine is still hot.

CHAPTER 28

What Can I Do if My Accelerator Pedal Gets Stuck?

1. I right away shift my gear to neutral.

2. Then, I try to unstick the pedal by pressing it hard and quickly releasing.

3. If this does not work, I try to use my foot to pull it up, using my toe.

4. If nothing works, I apply the foot brake and the emergency brake then I look for a way out of traffic flow, signal my intention to change lane, use my horn, and activate my four-way flasher to warn other drivers.

5. I stop as far as I can from the traveled portion of the road, with the four-way flasher on and early warning device deployed.

6. I get help and do not drive until the accelerator pedal is fixed.

Note

a. While the accelerator pedal is stuck and the vehicle is still moving, I will not turn the ignition key off; the power assist will be cut off, and this will increase steering and braking effort.

CHAPTER 29

What Causes Skidding and How to Avoid It

A. Skidding is due to any of the following:

1. Wet pavement

2. Loose gravel

3. Oily road

4. Muddy road

5. Ice or packed snow

6. Too much steering movement

7. Starting with a heavy foot on the gas pedal

8. Hard braking

B. What do I do to avoid skidding?

1. I avoid braking suddenly on any of the first five listed.

2. I apply the brake lightly but rapidly on any of the first five above.

3. I steer my vehicle in the direction the rear end is skidding and never oversteer.

4. I avoid lifting my foot suddenly from the accelerator and keep my clutch engaged if driving a standard vehicle.

C. Cornering skid is due to the following:

1. Vehicle's excessive speed

2. Poor condition of tires

3. Slope of the road

Note

a. The above are general guidelines only. Consult with the manufacturer of the vehicle.

CHAPTER 30

What I Do and How I Check Intersections with Traffic Lights

1. If I'm driving straight through, at about a block from the intersection and the light is green, the next thing I check is the pedestrian crosswalk sign. If *walk* is on, I know the green light is new; most probably, I will have enough time to cross before the yellow light comes on.

2. However, if the *don't walk* sign is on, the green light is *stale* or about to turn yellow. At about half a block from the intersection, I check traffic behind me. If it's heavy or they are close to me, I ease up on my gas pedal, tap, and cover my brake to force traffic behind to slow down and to warn them that I might stop; this is to avoid being rear-ended.

3. If the yellow light comes on, I am ready to stop and not beat the light. However, as I apply my brake, I have to check again traffic behind so my braking will be adjusted according to the situation behind me.

4. While waiting for the green light and being in the front, I keep checking the traffic situation, those that cross my path. As soon as the light changes, I am ready to proceed, but I continue checking traffic from left, ahead, and then right. I don't count by saying "thousand and one, thousand and two" without checking traffic. Visually checking traffic that can be in conflict with me is the only sure way to know if I am safe. Otherwise, I might go to where I am not planning to go yet.

5. While I'm at the intersection, I continue checking traffic on my left and right; somebody might try to beat the lights, or there could be an emergency vehicle approaching nearby. Also, if there's a vehicle big enough to cover my view to see clearly on one side, I don't pass the vehicle; somebody that I can't see might be racing the light.

Note

a. If I don't check whether I have a stale green or not, I will not know what to expect before going through an intersection controlled by traffic lights. I will either run a yellow or red light, brake suddenly, get hit from the back, or cause an accident. Worse, I can get hurt and my insurance premiums can increase.

b. If I know I have to stop at an intersection with red traffic lights or stop signs, why do I have to be in a hurry? To save gas and give the brake longer life, I start to slow down early. If the road surface is slippery, the more concerned I am. I must know how much pressure to apply on my brake to avoid being hit from the back.

CHAPTER 31

What I Do if I Have a Front Wheel Going Off the Pavement While Driving on the Right Lane

1. I have to be calm and grip my steering wheel firmly.

2. I take pressure off my gas pedal and apply light braking only.

3. When my vehicle is under control, I check the outside lane and my left blind spot for traffic condition.

4. When safe, I signal left and steer gently back onto the road while I still keep checking traffic behind for safety.

5. Once I am on the pavement, I check traffic behind using my rearview mirror so I can adjust my speed and distance to the vehicles behind.

Note

The following can contribute to a vehicle running off the road and causing deadly crashes:

a. When a driver is tired due to long-distance driving.

b. Not having enough rest or sleep.

c.   Driving over the speed limit or under the influence of illicit substances.

d.   Reading and/or doing something that takes away the driver's attention.

CHAPTER 32

What Should I Do if I Have a Headlight Failure?

1. First I slow down and then switch on my parking lights and my four-way flasher so other drivers or pedestrians are warned of my presence and predicaments.

2. Then I check and signal for a lane change in order to pull off the road and park as far as I can from the traveled portion.

3. At the side of the road, with my flasher on and early warning device deployed, I try to switch on the headlight by flicking the low and high beams a few times.

4. It is possible that one will still be working as they are on separate circuits.

Note

    a. I carry extra fuses of different amps and the tools for easy removal and installation, for headlight failure or other electrical challenges are mostly due to a burned fuse.

CHAPTER 33

What Should I Do if I'm Involved in an Accident?

1. I must remain at the scene and help prevent further injury to victims.

2. I make sure that all engines are off, emergency flashers are on, and early warning device is deployed.

3. I must give assistance to the injured, comfort the victims with warm blanket, apply first aid, not crowd victims, and no smoking nearby.

4. I report the accident to the police if somebody is injured or killed and/or if property damage exceeds the minimum allowed by the government.

5. I exchange insurance information, phone, driver's license, and plate and registration numbers with the other driver and report the accident to the police without delay.

6. I take pictures or sketch the accident, make notes on how it started, including the date, time, location, make, model, color, plate number, position of vehicles, weather condition, and damage on the other vehicle, and I notify my insurance as soon as possible.

7. I exchange names, phone, driver's license, and plate and registration numbers with witnesses.

8. I never discuss with the other driver who is at fault; I leave it to the police and my insurance.

9. I attach my name, phone, driver's license number, and insurance information to the damaged vehicle's windshield if the owner can't be located.

10. If I'm the first at the scene of the accident, I make sure other vehicles are not involved. I help call the police and ambulance; I give the accurate location and conditions of injured people.

11. Even though the other driver obviously made the driving error, I don't automatically make any judgment.

Note

a. I have to ask myself, what could I have done to avoid the accident? Even though it is not my fault, I must learn from it so that it should not happen again.

b. The reason is that if I am hurt physically or even killed, it still hurts me and my family; it does not matter who is at fault.

c. The government can suspend the driver's license and/or the vehicle's registration if the accident is not reported to the proper authority on time.

d. Every vehicle should have a first-aid kit, fire extinguisher, and early warning device.

CHAPTER 34

Why and What Can I Do to Prepare My Vehicle for Winter Driving?

A. Why?

    1. Temperatures are below freezing point

    2. Icy roads—hard to stop and start

    3. Limited visibility due to fog or blizzard

B. What to Check and Replace if Needed

    1. Battery and tires

    2. Radiator antifreeze level and strength

    3. Engine oil for winter grade

    4. All belts' tension and for wear and tear

    5. Headlights, signal lights, and other lights

    6. Heater, defroster, and thermostat

    7. Fluid level of brakes, windshield, and power steering

8. All filters and have an engine tune-up

9. All hoses for tightness and wear and tear

C. What I Carry in Winter, Especially for Long-Distance Driving

1. Ice scraper

2. Plastic bags

3. Matches

4. Imperishable food

5. Early warning device

6. Shovel

7. Broom

8. Jumper cable

9. Blankets

10. Toke

11. First-aid kit

12. Chain

13. Shovel

14. Candles

15. Mittens

16. Cell phone

17. Flares

18. Extra battery for flashlight and cell phone

19. Flashlight

20. Bucket

21. Scarf

22. Sleeping bag

23. Red cloth to use as flag

24. Drinking water

Note

a. My gas tank should be almost full so as not to run out of gas in case I get stuck.

b. I carry a bottle or two of gas line antifreeze and add one bottle for every fill-up.

CHAPTER 35

Why and What Contributes
to Good Visibility

1. Good visibility is as important as the brake as far as traffic safety is concerned. If I don't see clearly ahead where I am going, I can't prepare or react early enough to plan my defensive technique to avoid and help prevent an accident from happening.

2. Good visibility requires the following equipment in good working condition:

    a. Headlights

    b. Side mirrors, left and right

    c. Windshield wipers, front and back

    d. Defroster

    e. Water reservoir, full of windshield fluid

    f. Snow and frost removed from windshield

    g. Windshield, free of cracks

3. Weather conditions that contribute to poor visibility are the following:

    a. Raining

    b. Foggy

    c. Smoky

    d. Snowing

    e. Cloudy

    f. Nighttime

4. I use low beam on any of the above, at undivided or divided highways.

5. I also avoid looking directly at bright lights from oncoming traffic because I can be blinded by the glare. Instead I look down at the edge of my lane until we pass each other.

6. In areas where I can use high beam, I switch my light to low beam when I am about 150 meters behind any vehicle and when I am 300 meters from an oncoming vehicle.

7. I never wear sunglasses when driving at night or when visibility is poor, and I always drive within the range of my headlights.

B. PRINCIPLES OF DEFENSIVE DRIVING AND ACCIDENT AVOIDANCE TECHNIQUES

CHAPTER 1

As a Defensive Driver, I Promise

1. I will not let an accident happen if I have the last clear chance to avoid it even though I didn't start or cause the mistake. I know I can't expect to help everyone, but I can help some. If all drivers do their share and help prevent accidents of what is left in their driving life by being helpful, not a liability, it will be a good start.

2. I will not let other drivers decide the state of my health by refusing to help and rectify the situation if I have the last clear chance to avoid an accident. I can't insist on my right of way; I must help because nothing is more important than my health and safety.

3. I will not pretend to have not seen the other driver's mistake or predicament or, worse, refuse to help since I have not contributed or started the negative situation.

4. I will not cross a street without first checking my intersection sign and the sign of the traffic crossing my path to make sure signs are being followed by everyone so as to prevent me from going where I don't plan to go yet.

5. I will not sacrifice my safety or a police ticket, which can even be more expensive than a day's pay, just to meet an appointment or schedule.

6. I will not ride a power scooter or power chair on the street without an antenna and a flag at the end so drivers can see me easily and to inform them of my presence. I must also attach flashing red lights for night use.

7. I will not drive if I experience fatigue or stress, knowing that it will affect negatively my driving ability and the safety of all road users as we all depend on one another for safety.

8. I will not be that naive not to know that driving is a privilege that requires all drivers to conform to all traffic rules and regulations. That it is not my right, like the right to live and breathe fresh air. The government may take it away from me for any reason if they believe that it may compromise my safety and the public at large.

9. I will not blow my horn or show my middle-finger hand salute to drivers' insignificant mistakes or shortcomings, knowing that it can escalate to road rage. I also know that no one is immune to making mistakes. Maybe they have a legitimate reason. Besides, what if I lose one second? I will stop at the next traffic light anyway.

10. I will not respond negatively to the above situation that others have started by making a mountain out of a molehill, knowing that it will only make matters worse. I should also be man enough to accept my mistake, be sorry, and learn from it.

11. I won't drive without proper training or knowledge on defensive driving and accident avoidance techniques to help minimize or avoid traffic accidents. For the same reason, I will not work without my hard hat and steel-toe shoes if I'm a construction worker.

12. Without a lifeline, I will not also wash windows on high-rise buildings, climb tall trees, or do mountain climbing. The same thing in driving—my lifeline is to learn and be able to apply defensive driving and accident avoidance techniques whenever I am behind the wheel.

13. I will not sacrifice the future and/or the health of my family, my passengers, and me just to prove a point when I have the right of way; it takes only a few seconds to save me a lifetime of regret. I cannot be a Monday-morning quarterback if I am involved in an accident; it will not matter—what had happened can't be undone, but I must accept that I have contributed to it by not being able to prevent the collision.

14. I will not try to teach every driver but will give a break to those that do not drive the way I want them to, knowing that I could be old and

still haven't educated them all. So why even bother? Instead I will enjoy every minute of my driving, be nice, and be helpful to all road users.

15. I will not let other road users frustrate me, knowing that all they want is to control my emotions so they can steal my joy.

16. I will always analyze every driving situation, anticipate, and help other drivers whenever needed to prevent and avoid a possible collision.

17. I will not fight traffic jams—they are not irritation—or use my energy to question the delay, but use it as an opportunity and believe that it helps me to polish my patience and to accept things that I can't change.

18. I will not let anyone frustrate or control me when I am behind the wheel. I love everyone from a distance, even those I think have annoying habits or behaviors. I owe my forgiving and accommodating attitude to learning defensive driving and accident avoidance technique.

19. I will not cross a sidewalk from parking lots, back alleys, and/or driveways without first stopping before it to check left and right for pedestrians, motorized wheelchairs, and/or bicycle riders. As soon as I see a traffic break, but before I proceed forward, I check again the sidewalk because while I was checking for traffic opening, somebody could be using it ahead of me.

20. I will not do any texting or using my cell phone while I'm driving, not only because it's against the law but also because it makes me exhibit the same behavior as a drunk driver.

21. I will not be horn happy, blowing at every driver that makes a mistake. I do not want to be inconsiderate; instead I use it as an opportunity to be polite and to show empathy to fellow drivers or other road users because they are my friends I haven't met.

22. I will not forget to check my right side before I make a right turn to be sure it's clear of pedestrians and other sidewalk users. Since sidewalk users have the right of way, some, if not most, do not check for their safety before crossing. So the onus is on me, the driver, to make sure my turn is done safely.

23. I will not only check traffic, traffic lights, and/or turning arrows before I make a left turn but also check pedestrians and other road users. If I proceed to turn not knowing that the crosswalk is being occupied by pedestrians, I will either hit them or be forced to stop and block the lane of traffic that is heading toward me. I will be in trouble and cannot go anywhere except to pray and ask for divine intervention to help and save my soul.

24. I should not let my faith and desire for road safety be in words only; I have to learn defensive driving and accident avoidance techniques now. I don't wait for tomorrow, for tomorrow may never come. With defensive driving, I will be able to do my part to help make the roads safer. I know that we are all in this endeavor; we must not delay. Talk and promises are cheap. If I protect others, they in turn will protect me. We have had this carnage in the road for too long. Let us start to learn defensive driving and accident avoidance techniques. It's about time we do something.

25. I will not settle for good enough; it is just temporary, and I should not make it permanent that even though I'm good in handling my vehicle and follow rules and regulations, I could still be in conflict with other road users if I'm weak on defensive driving and accident avoidance techniques. I need the knowledge to prepare me for any weather or road conditions to avoid and prevent possible accidents.

CHAPTER 2

Drivers Are Mostly Polite, Only Some Have Bad Attitude

But Courteous At

1. Bank lines

2. Buffet lines

3. Restaurant lines

4. Medical office lines

5. Airport lines

6. Train lines

7. Shopping center lines

8. Lottery lines

9. Motor vehicle lines

10. Movie house lines

11. Government office lines

12. School campus lines

13. Bus lines

14. Cashier lines

15. Elevator lines

Note

a. But why do supposedly well-mannered individuals become so emotional and hot-tempered when behind the wheel, but are caring and helpful elsewhere?

b. The reason could be that one is not acquainted and/or trained on defensive driving.

CHAPTER 3

Drivers' Food for Thought

(Ideas are repeated for emphasis and because driving is a repetitious maneuver.)

1. Every driver should consider himself a bird or an airplane; for balancing and flying, two wings are needed. Likewise in driving, passing the road test is one wing. Learning defensive driving and accident avoidance techniques is the other wing. Without either, driving will not be safe.

2. One will never appreciate the advantage of learning defensive driving until a driver is in an accident. Be a part of the solution and not a part of the problem. A driver is judged by the ability to avoid an accident.

3. If I don't know how to notice an impending trouble or don't know how to help and prevent an accident, where will my dream be today if tomorrow I am involved in an accident that is not even my fault?

4. The best and lasting gift I can give to my family and myself is to learn defensive driving and accident avoidance techniques because there's no better present than a safe and healthy breadwinner.

5. I cannot be like others who constantly rationalize and justify their reason for delaying or not taking defensive driving. It is the only thing that can lessen road stress or accidents and have harmony with other drivers. I don't want to be like the other guy who is complaining of having aches and pains. When advised by a friend to go see a doctor, his answer was "I will go when I feel better."

6. That defensive driving and accident avoidance techniques are not one minute to midnight, but a long-term solution to road safety. Remember, accidents can deprive the breadwinner of the care and support they provide to loved ones.

7. That the safety in the road belongs to those who learn and know how to apply defensive driving and accident avoidance techniques. Don't ever think that learning defensive driving is a waste of time and money. Try a traffic accident?

8. That a driver without knowledge of defensive driving and accident avoidance techniques is the architect of his or her demise, if involved in an accident regardless of who is at fault. A responsible driver knows that self-preservation is the first law of nature.

9. Some drivers have the tendency to blame other drivers because they don't know the rule of having the last clear chance to avoid preventable accidents regardless of who has the right of way. In driving, one might lose one second but gain hours besides the thrill of being able to help and prevent a possible collision.

10. Due to the fact that the unexpected does happen, if one is not equipped with the solution, how do we expect to come out a winner?

11. Drivers have different abilities and/or states of mind as many as the number of drivers on the roads. Thus, defensive driving and accident avoidance techniques are necessary. Also, road and weather conditions do change. In driving, the defensive driver is king.

12. That if I drive especially in the city or where the road is busy,

   a. I drive one lane away from parked vehicles to have a space cushion;

   b. I leave the outside or curb lane free to make it easier for vehicles turning right at intersections or parking lots and safer for me because it saves me from changing lanes if the vehicle ahead turns right;

   c. if I'm following a vehicle that turns right and makes a sudden and hard stop because there's somebody using the sidewalk, I will rear-end the vehicle due to our failure to check and anticipate possible problem; and

d.   if I want to turn right at an intersection, I never activate my right signal before a vehicle that is trying to exit from the parking lot or back alley—they might think that I am turning where they are. If they move forward and I don't turn to the parking lot or back alley, a collision will surely happen.

13.   Remember that the roads are the paradise of bad drivers; the business opportunity for tow trucks, body shops, mortuaries, hospitals, insurance companies, and lawyers; but an unnecessary disruption to the police, courts, the people involved, and their family.

14.   Drivers with limited knowledge of defensive driving and accident avoidance techniques will never have all the necessary tools to be a safe and helpful driver. Even small or near-accidents will eventually escalate to an occasion that they and their loved ones will regret.

15.   I believe that I can only live and die once, and if I can't add more years to my life, at least I should add more driving fun to what is left of my driving days by learning to forgive, being helpful, and not answering negatively to provocative gestures of others as it could develop or escalate to road rage, a curse to one's well-being.

16.   Every minute of our waking hour, we do something to stop or abort possible accidents from happening. Likewise, every driver should have the same mentality as a babysitter; they don't wait for the child to be in trouble before they do something. The true measure of a defensive driver is judged by their ability to help prevent accidents.

17.   Going through one's life blaming other drivers for every driving challenge is the worst thing a driver can do. Only a foul person will not prepare for the unforeseen event; there's nothing certain in driving. Some accidents can't be avoided all the time, but without knowledge on defensive driving and accident avoidance techniques, it might be worse.

18.   There's an amount of dedication required to learn defensive driving and accident avoidance techniques. Remember that even half a defensive

driver is better than no defense at all. Don't just take the easy way out and blame the other driver.

19. Blaming others only if one is involved in an accident interferes with the ability to find what a person could have done to avoid it, since accidents are usually dual problems.

20. It is not mandatory to take defensive driving and accident avoidance techniques in order to get a driver's license, but for self-preservation and a great asset for safety. Just like lottery, one can only win if one buys. If a driver doesn't buy the idea of learning defensive driving, how do they know to spot, avoid, and/or help to prevent a collision?

21. A driver without knowledge of defensive driving and accident avoidance techniques may not realize

   A. that he or she is guilty of driving blindly and is a black sheep on the road;

   B. that it teaches the eyes to do more work than both the hands and feet together;

   C. that it is the mother of safe and courteous driving;

   D. that vehicles are deadly weapons if not used safely and defensively;

   E. that they finish the day's driving journey full of stress and without safety;

   F. that they have the tendency to aggravate other drivers' negative behavior that could escalate to becoming a victim of road rage;

   G. that it is much cheaper than being a maimed driver and attending physical therapy;

   H. that drivers have only one life or health and that it should be guarded at all costs;

   I. that it is the driver's parachute and safety net when behind the wheel;

J.   that some drivers don't always do the right thing, for whatever reason, but must be forgiven and helped (nobody is without mistake); and

K.   that having the necessary tools and the knowledge to be safe and helpful, one trained in defensive driving survives if confronted with hazardous driving conditions.

CHAPTER 4

Examples of Ground Rules Parents Should Have with Teen Drivers

1. Only daytime driving until further notice and call home upon reaching destination.

2. No passenger except members of the family and must be cleared with parents first.

3. No alcohol or drug of any kind—or even prescribed, if cautioned—when behind the wheel.

4. No driving during inclement weather without first being shown how and approved by parent.

5. Cannot drive without first getting approval from parents or when tired or upset.

6. Can only drive after giving the reason and approximate time to be home.

7. Can't move vehicle without first adjusting seat and mirrors and belts fastened by everybody.

8. Never listen to a request for anything against traffic rules or defensive driving procedures.

9. Start training for poor driving conditions as soon as possible.

10. Cell phone for emergency use while driving, but pull safely to the side of the road to use.

Note

Agreement with teen driver is a good start, but parents must set an example:

a. By following all traffic rules and regulations when behind the wheel.

b. By not swearing when other drivers make a mistake but instead helping regardless of who is at fault.

c. So everybody is on the same page on road safety, both parents and their teen driver should learn defensive driving and accident avoidance techniques.

CHAPTER 5

How Can I Be a Defensive Pedestrian?

I cross streets by doing the following:

1. Checking traffic left and right, even with flashing yellow crosswalk lights on.

2. Making sure the vehicle stops and having eye contact with the driver.

3. Continuing to check left and right while crossing to make sure of my safety.

4. Stopping before every open lane, if I'm covered by a stopped vehicle, to make sure I am safe.

5. Always checking for safety as health and life are preferable to right of way.

Reasons:

a. I can never win against a motor vehicle.

b. I can never entrust solely my safety to a motorist.

c. I can never depend on my right of way to guarantee my safety.

d. I know drivers don't intentionally make mistakes but are humans and can make mistakes.

Due to numerous things that the driver has to check like constantly changing traffic, pedestrian, lights' condition when visibility is poor, pedestrian's dark clothing—all contribute to a driver's error. Vehicle's windshield post can also cover a pedestrian.

The above is not to give excuses to drivers but to inform pedestrians that cooperation and understanding are the keys to safety.

In spite of government effort to lessen pedestrian accidents, there are still drivers that fail to follow traffic rules and regulations.

Statistics from NHTSA

1.   In 2010, 4,280—number of pedestrians that died in traffic crashes.

2.   In 2010, 70,000 pedestrians were injured—14,000 aged fourteen and younger; 8,000 were males.

3.   In 2009, 16 percent of all traffic fatalities in the United States were aged sixty-five and older.

Statistics from Wikipedia, the Free Encyclopedia

1.   The 32,367 traffic fatalities in 2011 were the lowest in sixty-two years (1949). On average in 2011, eighty-nine people were killed on the roadways of the United States each day.

2.   In 2010 there were an estimated 5,419,000 crashes, killing 32,885 and injuring 2,239,000.

Statistics from United States Military Casualties of War
(Wikipedia, the Free Encyclopedia)

			Total Death	Death/Year	Death/Month
1.	World War II US combat death	1941-45	291,557.00	58,311.40	4,859.28
	US traffic death	1941-45	137,826.00	27,565.20	2,297.10
2.	Korean War US combat death	1950-53	33,746.00	8,436.50	703.04
	US traffic death	1950-53	140,773.00	35,193.25	2,932.77
3.	Vietnam War	1955-75	47,424.00	2,371.20	197.60
	US traffic death	1955-75	940,659.00	47,032.95	3,919.41

Total US traffic death during the above three wars—1,219,258

Total US combat death during the above three wars—372,727

Some Drivers' Situations or Conditions That Can Distract
to Contribute to Pedestrian Accidents

1. Drinking and/or eating

2. Grooming

3. Using cell phone

4. Being intoxicated

5. Having physical challenges

6. Playing loud music

7. Smoking and/or reading

8. Being in a bad weather or road condition

9. Reaching behind

CHAPTER 6

How Can I Reduce Vehicle Insurance?

1. By taking or learning defensive driving and accident avoidance techniques.

    a. It teaches me to be more responsible, caring, forgiving, and courteous. This lowers the number of accidents and traffic tickets, making the roads safer, resulting in lowering insurance premiums.

    b. The length of a driver's experience does not define a safe driver; defensive driving and accident avoidance techniques do. It shows how to prevent and avoid an accident regardless of who's at fault.

    c. Not only is insurance lowered but camaraderie is also instilled to every driver out there, because they are all our brothers or sisters, only from a different mother.

2. It reviews traffic rules and regulations and reasons for not procrastinating or making excuses to justify delaying to learn defensive driving, as safety overrides excuses and is also better on the pocketbook.

    a. Safety in the road belongs to those who learn defensive driving and accident avoidance techniques and apply them without reservation; safety is always better than the best cure.

    b. So why not improve the odds to be on the side of safety? Accidents can happen to any driver.

c. Defensive driving is every driver's interest, because one day it will make sense to somebody that has an accident, realizing that the collision could have been prevented, having the last clear chance to avoid the accident.

3. By not having heavy conversation with passengers, using handheld cell phone to call or text, playing loud music, and smoking.

   a. All of the above can contribute to traffic accidents as they distract the driver's attention.

   b. Texting and using a cell phone while driving may have the same consequences as that of a drunk driver, and if one is in an accident, the financial impact to the driver and his family will be serious and expensive.

4. No DUI or possession of illicit drugs and maintains average yearly miles of twelve to fifteen thousand.

   a. Traffic tickets and lawyer's fees are costly, and imprisonment disrupts not only the driver's life but also the whole family. Also, profession, employment, and earning power are affected.

5. Single male or female driver, twenty-five years old or younger:

   a. Must maintain a good driving record—no speeding, moving violations, and/or accidents regardless of who is at fault. To help further improve driving skills, one must take and learn defensive driving and accident avoidance techniques.

   b. It not only lowers or maintains insurance fees but also protects their health, which sometimes they think is not everything, but when they lose it, they realize that they lose everything.

6. Other Ways to Lower Vehicle Insurance

   a. Shop around and compare; let the fingers do the walking.

   b. Inquire about higher deductibles and group insurance.

   d. Insure home, auto, or apartment together.

e. Inquire about coverage for older vehicles.

f. Find out how to have a high credit score.

g. Take advantage of low-mileage discount.

CHAPTER 7

How I Apply Traffic Rules and Safety Procedures

1. That I signal with sufficient time to provide a reasonable warning to other drivers and other road users of what I plan to do.

2. That I must signal and check my blind spots before I move out from a parking space or curb.

3. That I must not activate my signal too early or too late or forget to turn it off when my maneuver is finished so as not to confuse my fellow drivers, which can easily start an accident.

4. That I must not pass a vehicle that has stopped or slowed down at marked or unmarked crosswalks. I have to assume that there's a reason for their action. Somebody may be crossing that is hidden by the stopped vehicle. So I must slow down, check, and be ready to stop.

5. That I must stop and check from left to right before pedestrian crosswalks, from service roads, back alleys, driveways, and/or parking lots prior to entering the main street.

6. That when I am approaching a road where there's an emergency situation, construction site, or maintenance area, I must be on the lookout for danger, exercise caution, and follow the instruction of the flagger that is responsible for directing traffic.

7. That when I come close to an emergency situation or police-initiated stop, I must continue to concentrate on my driving task, slow down, and if possible, drive one lane away from the stopped emergency vehicle.

8. That I must not insist on my right of way but drive defensively and help avoid an accident, having the last clear chance, regardless of who is at fault. Why should I refrain from helping when doing this benevolent act is for my benefit too?

9. That I must continually seek to improve my defensive driving skills; it is the law of life. If I am only contented with being a mediocre driver, for sure, I will miss the best of driving. I know that every man is the architect of his own safety and emotional condition while behind the wheel.

CHAPTER 8

How I Avoid Anger and Road Rage When Behind the Wheel

1. I set my alarm clock fifteen to thirty minutes earlier than what I need to prepare myself, the expected travel time plus unexpected events.

2. I make a checklist of what to do for the next day, what to prepare, and also a reminder on what to do on the way back home, if any.

3. I gather all the things needed and put them in a box, like clothes to wear, keys, shoes, glasses, a watch, jewelry, a hat, and/or lunch, in a convenient and safe place.

4. I give special attention and check regularly the fuel, oil, tire pressure, radiator fluid, and belts for proper tension to have a vehicle that is operationally ready so as not to be a hazard to others and to myself, if I have car trouble on the road.

5. I just relax if I'm still late due to traffic accidents caused by others, detours, and/or construction. There's nothing more I can do, and I must accept that there are things that are beyond my control.

6. I should not speed up if I am late, because I can be more delayed by having an accident or speeding ticket, which can be even more expensive than the day's salary. If I have an appointment and I happen to be late, I can easily reschedule it.

CHAPTER 9

How I Demonstrate and What to Tell My Children about the Way to Cross Streets

A.   At an Intersection with Traffic Lights

   1.   I show them where the crosswalk switch is located and where to stand, not too close to the edge of the road, and to keep observing traffic.

   2.   I tell them to check traffic first before starting to cross, even when the *walk* sign had come on, to make sure that vehicles have stopped.

   3.   Before we cross, I hold their hands and walk briskly—no running—and with full attention to safety.

   4.   We pause and check at every lane that is vacant or open as we continue checking traffic from left to right. Drivers may not realize that a pedestrian is crossing and hidden.

B.   At a pedestrian crosswalk, I emphasize the following:

   1.   To apply the above procedures at pedestrian crosswalks with flashing yellow lights or only painted white lines.

   2.   That the only safe place to cross is where there's a pedestrian crosswalk and that if they cross anywhere else, their health or life could be in danger.

3. I show the above procedures a few times, then whenever we go out, to make sure every safety precautions are followed, I let my children take turns being the leader when crossing and explain what to do.

4. That they should not horseplay, push, or run but concentrate on checking traffic left and right and never be influenced by negative behaviors of others.

5. To give a hand signal to show to drivers that one wants to cross, but wait for the driver to acknowledge it and to cross only after the vehicle has stopped.

6. To wear something that is visible—no black at night or during inclement weather.

7. To wait for the vehicle to completely stop before proceeding to cross. Never assume the driver has seen you, not until there's eye contact.

8. To never use a cell phone to call, text, and/or answer calls while crossing the road.

9. That even though a pedestrian has the right of way when crossing properly, the pedestrian is always the loser if in an accident, because the human body can't win against a moving vehicle that can result in losing one's life or being maimed physically.

Note

a. I believe that there's too much emphasis given on right of way. We forget that health and life are at stake. We should caution and warn pedestrians that for every right, there's a corresponding responsibility—that is to protect our self from harm.

C. An Example of an Accident while Crossing a Crosswalk with Flashing Yellow Lights

A mother with three young girls—ages five, seven, and nine—were crossing a street with flashing yellow lights. They were going to a fast-food restaurant; the girls were so jubilant like most young people at their age.

Since they were crossing at a crosswalk with flashing yellow lights, the mother was so confident and let the three girls cross ahead of her without first checking for safety.

A young male at the same time was driving with his girlfriend. Just before reaching the crosswalk where the three girls and the mother were, he kissed his girlfriend a little bit longer than he should; unaware of the situation in front, he ran over two of the young girls.

Note

    a.   The mother should have held their hands, stopped at the edge of the road, and double-checked for safety, even with yellow flashing lights, before starting to cross. She should have led the way and continued checking for safety while they were crossing.

D.   Second Example of a Pedestrian Accident

This young girl from school was somewhat in a hurry to reach home and ran to cross the street from the front of the bus.

At the same time, a male driver who was driving behind the bus made a quick lane change and tried to pass without slowing down or checking for pedestrians that might be crossing in front of the bus.

The combination of a pedestrian in a hurry to cross and a driver passing a bus without precaution is dangerous. Obviously, the young girl was badly hurt.

Note

    a.   Before passing a vehicle that had stopped, one should take precautions to be ready for any eventuality by covering the brake and checking the inside rearview mirror to see if a vehicle is following close behind to avoid being rear-ended. Next as you move slowly, keep checking the front of the vehicle for pedestrians.

    b.   If the vehicle being passed is other than a bus, I check the inside of the vehicle to see if there's a driver. They might open their door or move the vehicle forward without first checking for safety. Or there could be a passenger at the backseat that might open the roadside door for exit.

c. Another safety precaution as an early warning strategy is, from a distance, drivers must check under the vehicle; if a foot is seen, it is a sign that a pedestrian is present but hidden.

d. A bus that stops to pick up or drop passengers has contributed lots of accidents mainly due to pedestrians crossing either from the front or back and not checking first for safety—worse if they run, giving the driver no time to react. Drivers must anticipate and be prepared for pedestrians that might be hidden due to the size of the bus. "A few seconds of precaution may save a lifetime of regret."

E. Third Example of a Pedestrian Accident

A mother picks her child from a babysitter. They have to cross the street from the middle of a block, using a stroller. A vehicle from the outside lane stops to let her cross, but she forgets to stop and check the next lane. Since the driver in the next lane sees no pedestrians yet, he does not slow down or take precautions. You guess it: mother and child are hit.

Note

a. Pedestrians should never assume that if a vehicle stops in one lane to let them cross, that drivers in the other lanes will automatically stop; a nondefensive driver will not. Pedestrians have to check the next lane separately before crossing, for their safety.

b. Drivers should always assume that a pedestrian can be shielded by a parked, stopped, or even slow-moving vehicle. They should slow down and prepare to stop by checking the rearview mirror and covering the brake while checking the front of the vehicle they are passing.

CHAPTER 10

How to Pass Driving Road Test

1. First and foremost, one should be confident; if not, you are not ready—a sign of lack of skill and need for more practice.

2. Be familiar with the vehicle you are going to use, and drive it a few times to know how it behaves. Know how to check the blind spots, the locations of instruments and their use, and how to adjust mirrors, seats, and the headrest.

3. Know how to sit comfortably and how to hold the steering wheel properly, either nine and three or two and ten o'clock. Never use one hand only; use hand over hand for turning and no palming. Stop and start smoothly.

4. Know the proper way to check before any maneuver, in this order:

    a. Check inside mirror and shoulder or blind spot; if not safe, repeat it.

    b. If it is safe, signal intention, but keep checking traffic behind for safety.

    c. Where to check and the signal depend on what one wants to do.

5. Before one stops or starts, turns left or right, or changes lane, always do all the steps above for safety. Also, never forget to cancel signal after the maneuver.

6. Before one backs up for any reason, take the proper sitting position. Never move the vehicle until after checking behind for safety. Check first straight behind the vehicle, then on the right and left sides. If clear, look directly behind, move slowly, stop, and repeat the checking and stopping as you back up slowly.

7. At stop signs, stop completely before pedestrian crosswalks, imaginary or not, before checking pedestrians and traffic from left, ahead, and right. Repeat the checking as many times as needed, depending on traffic volume, as you move forward.

8. If one has a yield sign, drive slowly while at the same time checking traffic at the intersection from all directions. Yield or stop if there's traffic or a pedestrian that is close-by.

9. If the intersection has no sign for you but the traffic crossing your path has a yield or stop sign, still be very careful, and make sure they give you your right of way.

10. If the intersection is uncontrolled, check all directions as you move slowly forward.

11. At school zones, never drive faster than the speed limit posted, and be ever watchful for students that might be crossing.

12. While doing general driving, you don't only check for vehicles but also for pedestrians that might be crossing legally or illegally and for speed limits. Give pedestrians courtesy and their right of way.

13. Be careful when driving close to parked vehicles; pedestrians could be hidden. Check the inside of vehicle; driver could move forward, or pedestrians might use the roadside to exit without first checking for safety.

14. For parallel parking, don't memorize the steps by counting the number of turns and lining doors and bumpers. This is a sign that you still don't know the principles of backing. Learn backing by practicing in a quiet area. You should be able to park by just looking and lining your vehicle at the one behind.

15. For hill parking, again don't memorize which way to turn, but know the reason you turn the wheels.

16. Before you reach the intersection, you should have checked the signs for you and for the traffic crossing to know what to do and what to expect from the other driver. If in doubt about your safety, help even if it's your right of way. You only need a second to rectify a possible collision, but you prevent a lifetime of regret.

Note

a. Even though it is cheaper at the outset if one practices with somebody that is not a driving instructor, but it could be more expensive later.

b. An instructor is preferable, if one can afford, but it is expensive too. For the price of less than an hour of professional help, you can have *1001 Ways to Drive Defensively* that you and your family can share as reference.

CHAPTER 11

I Must Emulate Some Behaviors
of a Soldier in Operation

1. Always check and know what is happening around me when I'm behind the wheel.

2. Be ready to help, avoid, and prevent vehicle and pedestrian conflict at any given time.

3. Check and analyze any action that drivers or pedestrians are doing or planning to do, to make sure that our safety is not compromised.

4. Check and follow all traffic rules and regulations as safety overrides excuses.

5. Anticipate and prepare the defensive solution to any developing traffic problem, regardless of who has the right of way.

Note

a. Safety should be always first in my mind before right of way, by applying the above techniques that men in uniform conduct in their mission.

CHAPTER 12

Motor Vehicle Theft Prevention Precautions from NHTSA

1. Park in well-lighted areas, and don't leave the registration or title in the vehicle.

2. Always lock the vehicle, and replace easily-accessible door lock assemblies.

3. Park in attended lots if possible, and never hide a second set of keys in the vehicle.

4. Do not leave valuables in plain sight, and completely close all windows when parking.

5. Leave only the ignition and door key if parked in an attended lot.

6. Never leave the vehicle running even if only gone for a minute.

7. Park with wheels turned toward the curb to make the vehicle more difficult to tow away.

8. Backing into the driveway will make it more difficult for the thief to tow away the vehicle if its rear wheel drives.

9. Garage the vehicle if one have, and always remember to lock the garage door.

10. To ensure safety and also make it difficult for a thief to tow away the vehicle, when parking, engage the emergency brake.

11. To trace vehicle and its parts easily when stolen, etch the identification number on the windows and major parts.

12. Disable the vehicle when leaving it unattended for an extended period of time.

13. Engrave one's date of birth on car stereos, cellular phones, compact disc changers, and external speakers so that the thief will have difficulty disposing of expensive accessories.

14. To help assist law enforcement in identifying the vehicle or its parts, drop business cards, address labels, or other identifications inside the vehicle's door.

15. Install an antitheft device or system on the vehicle as an extra deterrent measure.

CHAPTER 13

Safety and Statistics Every Driver Should Know

Whenever I am behind the wheel, whether I live in a big city and/or small town, there's always the inherent risk of being involved in an accident. It is the purpose of this book, *1001 Ways to Drive Defensively*, to educate drivers on the different defensive driving and accident avoidance techniques that drivers can use to help lower the chance of getting involved in an accident, regardless of who has the right of way or who has initiated it.

Statistically, the most at risk of getting into traffic accidents, more than any age group, are the young drivers.

Older drivers, due to slow reaction time, poor hearing or vision, and some other physical impairment, have a high risk of getting involved in traffic accidents.

Also, the vehicle we drive plays a big factor when it comes to safety. To protect our lives, limbs, passengers, investments, and other road users, regular maintenance and inspection for the proper operation of the vehicle are very important.

I remind myself of the following before I start my vehicle:

1. To be courteous and helpful to all road users that need my assistance.

2. To be forgiving to the mistakes of others; I too make mistakes.

3. To help avoid accidents via defensive driving regardless of who is at fault.

4. To observe and adjust my driving to changing traffic and weather condition.

Note

    a. All drivers are urged to learn defensive driving and accident avoidance techniques as most accidents are preventable regardless of who has the right of way.

"Don't forget—you're protecting the most expensive thing that even all the money in the world can't replace."

CHAPTER 14

Since Drivers Are Humans and Can Make Mistakes

1.   I should be kind and make allowances for their mistakes or shortcomings; only then can I enjoy my driving.

2.   I don't wait for other drivers to correct their mistakes or adjust to bad conditions. Time is of the essence. I help to correct the negative situation and not insist on my right of way. We are both in danger, plus the other driver may not realize the impending danger or have the knowledge to fix the negative condition.

3.   I must learn early that it is not my duty to change the other driver's behavior, nor can I expect them to do the right thing all the time. I can only expect the best, but I must be prepared to help, if needed, by applying defensive driving and accident avoidance techniques.

4.   I must be vigilant, be helpful, and never lose my temper when I'm behind the wheel, regardless of who has the right of way or who made the driving error. Having the knowledge of defensive driving and accident avoidance techniques gives me the solution and the confidence with no hostility toward other drivers. Instead I feel good for being able to help and at the same time save myself from trouble.

5.   I start to develop good driving behavior by helping and forgiving the mistakes of other drivers, which eventually will influence others to do

the same thing, just as I instill good driving attitudes to my children by example.

6. I must accept that there are drivers that are like toxic truck drivers driving all over town, looking for where to dump their load. I don't let them dump it on me and be the recipient of their garbage. I always remind myself that I should act like an eagle—they don't fight crows; they just soar high up in the sky and resume with their mission.

CHAPTER 15

Some Behave Like Toxic Truck Drivers Looking Where to Empty Their Load

I have to be vigilant, be defensive, and not let them make me the recipient of their unwanted load; otherwise,

a. they can change a relaxing day and decide the kind of emotion I will have;

b. they steal my joy and good nature—makes me less defensive and less helpful;

c. they can affect my positive relationship with those close to me and/or my colleagues;

d. they make me forget to plant seeds of kindness—not only my duty but also my responsibility;

e. they make me lose the pleasure of driving and forget to look for an opportunity to be kind; and

f. they make me behave the way they want instead of what I wish for.

Note

a. Only knowledge of defensive driving can override negative behaviors of other drivers.

b. One will notice that after learning defensive driving, all the annoying habits and behaviors of other drivers seem to have disappeared.

CHAPTER 16

Sometimes There Are Two Kinds of Drivers

(The Person at the Wheel and the So-Called Backseat Driver)

1.   The second driver is called the backseat driver, or BSD—not directly in control of the vehicle but eager to give criticisms or suggestions to the driver's action or lack of it.

2.   The BSD is uncomfortable and doesn't feel safe with the driver's way of driving; thus, he or she has to tell what the driver should do but usually washes his/her hands if an accident happens.

3.   The problem with the BSDs is that they are constantly giving unsolicited advice and criticism and are rather argumentative and bossy, which makes the driver confused and more erratic.

Note

Backseat drivers come into existence because the driver does not show knowledge on defensive driving and is late in telegraphing that he or she has recognized a possible problem by showing it through action that is visible and understood by the BSD, like

   a.   if a potential problem exists, the driver is late in covering or applying the brakes and does not check the rearview mirror to know the situation behind for safety;

b.   if driver is not adjusting speed to the condition of the road, the weather, at intersections, stop signs, red lights, school zones, and playgrounds;

c.   if driver doesn't check mirrors or blind spots and signal when turning, changing lanes, or stopping and/or does not cancel signal when maneuver is finished.

d.   Backseat drivers usually have good intentions; they add more eyes and skills if done properly, but it should not become a routine or be overdone. However, a BSD or a driver's assistant is needed or mandatory for long and night driving.

e.   If the driver doesn't understand the reason behind the criticism, it is a warning sign to learn defensive driving and accident avoidance techniques.

CHAPTER 17

The Basic Parking Rules that I Follow

A. I never park on the following:

1. On the traveled portion of the road and within fifty feet of the nearest rail of a railroad.

2. On curves, near intersections, on hills, and where parking is prohibited.

3. To block sidewalks or crosswalks, in front of private or public garages, and/or at driveways.

4. Less than nine feet from fire hydrants, double-park, or opposite any vehicle.

5. Next to or opposite a highway construction zone.

6. In a space reserved for handicapped unless I have a permit, but I must observe for "van parking only."

7. Close to any bridge and within highway tunnels.

Note

a. If parking is allowed on the outside lane of the road, the driver and passengers must first check vehicles, bicycles, and pedestrians from behind before the door next to traffic is opened.

b. Passengers are to exit on the curbside—it's safer and preferred.

CHAPTER 18

The Consequences of Traffic Accidents

A.   Here are some:

1.   The deterioration of one's health

2.   Changing of one's goal

3.   Having a financial problem

4.   Changing one's hobby

5.   Limited connection to relatives or friends

6.   Frequent visits to doctors or hospitals

7.   The curtailment of social events

8.   Lowering of one's self-worth

9.   Loss of mobility and/or freedom

10. Loss of intimacy with one's love

11. The premature loss of one's life

12. Losing one's pride

13. The waste of valuable time

14. Changing or lowering the standard of one's lifestyle

15. Constant aches and pains

16. Lots of and frequent medications

17. Loneliness and the loss of joyful life

18. Substance abuse

19. Feeling depressed

20. Having a short fuse

B. What then should a driver do?

1. Contrary to some beliefs that accidents happen without warning, they do come with a short window of warning or sign, which every defensive driver should be able to recognize quickly and apply the necessary defensive move or exit strategy regardless of who is at fault.

2. Whoever has the last clear chance should be ready and willing to help without insisting on one's right of way. Review the consequences of having an accident above. It does not matter whether one has the right of way or not; a broken bone still hurts the same way. One could scream and tell the whole world that it is somebody's fault, but it will not reverse anything. One will still feel the aches and pains and suffer the consequences that come with a traffic accident. Also, blaming others interferes with one's ability to find what one could have done.

3. Pretend that you are assigned to be a weather person but never went to school to study about it. Do you think you will be able to predict and warn the population about the coming of a cyclone, tornado, typhoon, rain, and/or the temperature of the day?

4. Likewise, in driving, if one has only limited knowledge on defensive driving and accident avoidance techniques, how can one

see, predict, avoid, and/or help rectify another driver's mistakes when one is not well schooled in defensive driving?

5.   Most drivers involved in an accident believe it happened without warning. This is never 100 percent the case. Actually, the driver never recognizes the situation that is developing. That can lead to a collision due to lack of knowledge on defensive driving. Or even the driver sees the situation that is gradually unfolding that can result into vehicle conflict but refuses to help, again because they believe that it is not their fault.

6.   Knowledge of defensive driving and accident avoidance techniques is the only thing that can protect a driver from collision. It could be due to human error, the weather, or road condition, but having learned defensive driving, one is knowledgeable on observing, avoiding, and helping other drivers or pedestrians stay away from an accident.

7.   Self-initiated defensive driving is started on the part of the driver, not by waiting for the other driver to fix their mistake or adjust to the unsafe condition, because they might not realize it, see it, or know what to do to eliminate the possible driver conflict.

8.   It is well-known that the roads are full of challenges. If you consider yourself a responsible driver and want to be a part of the solution, study and learn defensive driving and accident avoidance techniques without delay unless you prefer to be a part of the problem. It is a choice, however, in the name of safety for all, and I hope every driver learns and becomes a defensive driver to help lower the accidents in the roads we all travel.

9.   It has been proven many times that accidents can happen to even the so-called good driver, so why do some people don't improve the odds to be on the side of safety by taking and/or learning defensive driving and accident avoidance techniques? It is also well-known that collision plays havoc not only to the driver's health but also to their financial condition. One's safety overrides excuses for delaying to learn defensive driving.

10. Many drivers experience so little fun while behind the wheel, not because they don't know how to drive, but because they do

not have the knowledge to notice the situations that can lead to a vehicle conflict before it happens or know the defense or refuse to help because it is their right of way. Only learning defensive driving and accident avoidance techniques can and will provide a driver the necessary knowledge and proper driving attitude.

11. Many drivers think learning defensive driving and accident avoidance techniques is expensive or a waste of time; try an accident. Defensive driving overrides excuses and is the foundation that makes safe driving possible, which is not appreciated by most until one is in an accident.

12. A driver that has learned defensive driving and accident avoidance techniques doesn't just blame or tell the other driver what they should have done to avoid the accident. Instead, they ask themselves what they could have done to prevent the collision. This is because one can never control the other driver's action, which is affected by their physical or mental condition and other contributing factors that make them fail to follow traffic rules and regulations. In other words, we should not let our safety depend on other drivers or road users.

CHAPTER 19

The Following Situations Can Start an Accident or Road Rage

1. Driver *A* is driving faster than the speed limit and/or condition of the road; the possible reasons could be that

   ✓ A. driver *A* is trying to make up for starting late to an appointment or work;

   B. driver *A* didn't make an allowance for unforeseen events; or

   C. driver *A* could be emotionally upset.

   What should I do if I am the other driver?

   ✓ a. I stay out of his or her way.

   b. I don't do anything to aggravate the situation.

   c. I make sure that I am not driving below speed limit or condition of the road, so I I don't contribute to the driver's behavior.

2. Driver *B* is driving below speed limit or condition of the road; the possible reasons could be that

   A. there could be something wrong mechanically with the vehicle;

B.   driver *B* could have physical or age-related challenges; or

C.   driver *B* could be new in the area and/or looking for an address.

What should I do if I'm the other driver?

✓a.   I give the driver a break, make a lane change without being upset or blowing my horn, and let the police handle the situation.

b.   I just convince myself that the driver must have a good reason that I don't know.

3.   Driver *C* stops for a red light, is in front of the line, and does not move forward as soon as the green light comes on; the following are possible reactions from drivers behind:

a.   If I am one of them, I will wait for a while.

✓b.   Some will blow their horns right away and react with anger.

The following are possible reactions of driver *C* as a result of the negative behavior from behind:

✓a.   Accept the mistake, move forward quickly, and ignore the horn blowing behind.

b.   Blow the horn, raise fist, or give the middle-finger hand salute to show displeasure.

c.   Drive slower than required to antagonize the drivers behind.

Note

✓a.   If driver *C* was constantly checking pedestrians and traffic while waiting for the green lights, he or she should have been able to proceed without delay.

b.   Driver *C* should accept his or her shortcoming and show it by being sorry and not by trying to get even.

✓c.   Drivers behind should restrain their emotions; if the front vehicle is late for one second or two, sometimes they have a good reason for the delay, which drivers behind don't see or know.

4.   Driver *D* is driving an RV or an older vehicle below speed limit or condition of the road on a two-lane, winding, or mountainous road. This has created a long line of vehicles following; the following are possible reactions of drivers behind:

✓a.   A defensive driver will wait for an ideal location and situation before passing.

b.   Other drivers who are in a hurry may try to pass from a long line of traffic.

The following is a possible situation that could happen:

a.   If a vehicle from the opposite direction appears, it's inevitable that a deadly head-on collision could happen.

Note

a.   If a driver decides to take chances by making a lane change and another vehicle is coming from the opposite direction, I will adjust my speed to help and give room for the driver to return back to the lane.

b.   On the same situation above, if nobody helps and if collision cannot be avoided, for me, I would rather have a collision with the vehicles going in the same direction as opposed to head-on, or I steer to the ditch if it is not that deep.

✓c.   As a defensive driver, I know that "a few seconds may save a lifetime of regret," so I don't take chances. What good is it if I gain a minute or two but lose my health or my life?

5.   When driver *D* makes a fast lane change and dangerously cuts off another driver, the possible reasons are the following:

✓a.   The driver that was just passed may be driving below posted speed limit or condition of the road, and driver *D* is showing his/her displeasure.

b. The driver being passed speeds up instead of helping, or he or she may have done something that driver D doesn't appreciate.

c. Driver D may be a show-off or doesn't know how to change lanes properly.

Below are possible reactions from other drivers:

a. If I am the driver that was passed, to not give reason for other drivers to get upset, I drive according to the posted speed limit or condition of the road.

b. If somebody cuts me off dangerously, I ignore it and am thankful that nothing negative has happened, or I get the license number and report it to the police.

✓ c. As a defensive driver, I know that other drivers don't always do what is right, but I must forgive and help rectify the mistake. I'm not always without mistake either.

d. Other drivers may get agitated and retaliate and give the same treatment, which can start road rage. I believe that it is better to ignore any negative behavior.

Note

a. Retaliating on bad behaviors of other drivers is inviting trouble, and it's not worth it.

b. I will avoid reacting in a negative way, like giving a middle-finger hand salute, because it will be an invitation to escalate it further.

6. When driver E has the right signal on but is not changing lanes or turning, the following are possible reasons why the signal is on:

a. Driver E probably has just made a lane change and forgotten to put the signal off.

b. The driver's attention is focused on something else, and he is not concentrating on his driving.

What could be the result?

    a.   Drivers will be confused, and those coming from the right side, seeing the right signal, move forward. If driver *E* doesn't turn right, an accident is possible.

Note

    a.   Drivers from the right side of the road must not automatically expect that driver *E* will turn right because the right signal is on.

    b.   The following are sure signs that driver *E* is really turning:

        1.   The vehicle must be slowing down.

        2.   The driver must show that he or she is checking for a right turn.

        3.   The front tires of the vehicle must have started to turn to the right, and again, the driver must be checking the right side for safety.

7.   When driver *F* has an accident at an intersection, the following are the possible reasons:

    a.   Driver *F* did not check the intersection properly for signs and conditions.

    b.   Driver *F* didn't bother to double-check to confirm that it is really safe, upon seeing that he or she has the right of way.

    c.   Driver *F*'s eyes might have been bothered by the glare of the sun.

    d.   Driver *F* may not have slowed down to compensate for the road condition.

Note

    a.   For safety, driver *F*, even though he has the right of way, must still double-check all intersections.

b.   Driver *F*, regardless of the right of way, must have the right speed to negotiate and check properly the intersection for the presence of other road users.

c.   Right of way does not guarantee safety. Safety depends on drivers following traffic rules and regulations, driving defensively, and adjusting speed to the road and weather condition.

CHAPTER 20

The Law of Attraction in Driving

1. I believe that I attract what I am entertaining in my mind. So I only consider positive thoughts, like a safe and worry-free driving experience to work or an appointment. So in other words, I can lead my mind to believe what I want to entertain.

2. I believe and trust that all drivers are responsible and that I have no reason not to get along with everyone. If something happens that I do not agree with, I know it is an honest mistake on their part, not intended to aggravate me. Besides, my defensive driving skill is ever ready if I need to help.

3. I believe that thoughts can lead to anger or joy, so I shift my emotions when I drive to attract excitement, a happy feeling, care, cooperation, and a healthy attitude.

4. I believe very convincingly that my fellow road users will do their driving best, but I must not be too complacent, and I must be prepared for anything because human beings are involved. So I cannot be too lazy to help or insist on my right of way regardless of who is at fault.

5. I believe that helping other drivers through defensive driving speaks the language of love, thus making me a part of the solution and not a part of the driving problem.

6. I believe that the true measure of a good driver is not the one that blows their horn or gives a middle-finger hand salute to others' mistakes or misjudgment.

7. I believe that drivers that drive fast and change lanes for no apparent reason are a menace to the driving public and to themselves.

8. I believe that a responsible driver is one who does not get emotional or irritated when things don't go one's way and one that has the courtesy to give drivers from parking lots the chance to go ahead of them and to show appreciation by a simple thank-you gesture when appropriate.

9. I believe that uncaring drivers are those that will not help other drivers and cooperate when there's a merging lane ahead, because it is their right of way. They are not concerned in the event that an accident can be the result, which every responsible driver should avoid.

10. I believe that drivers who refuse to let others make a lane change are not well versed on the principles of defensive driving, as if they will lose their manhood if they do. It's not worth the aggravation for a simple act of kindness and cooperation.

11. I believe that if I continually cultivate a good relationship with my fellow drivers by giving them a break when needed, looking for an opportunity to help, trying to show kindness and patience, and applying defensive driving techniques, I will be rewarded with more than I give.

12. I believe that whatever I continually say is what I get. So I say the words in the direction of where I want, like "Today is going to be a great driving day for me."

13. I believe that if I give the other drivers an outlet to redeem their mistake by applying defensive driving techniques, not by insisting on my right of way, I get more mileage out of it.

14. I believe that if somebody makes a mistake, I must help as much as I can regardless of who is at fault so that I don't become the recipient of their mistake. My job is not to pull the weeds; instead, I just bloom with good attitude and am helpful.

15. I believe that I should not try to collect driving debt if somebody causes an accident or does something wrong, because I will only hurt myself if I try and get even with another mistake.

16. I believe that when I am confronted with some uncomfortable driving situation, I know it is to prepare me for some future negative events. So with a delay, an accident, or anything negative that happens, I face it calmly. I share the pain with those involved but should know not to spread it and cause more pain to others.

17. I believe that I should not probe who I am by being upset at other road users' mistakes. Instead, I help. Why, you ask? Because who else is more interested in keeping my health and sanity? I too have a responsibility for everybody's safety.

18. I believe that if it is to be, it is up to me. When I drive, I can choose to be happy and helpful, or I can choose to be easily irritated. I know that every day has a gift for my benefit; nobody can take it unless I am willing to give it away.

19. I believe that my failure to avoid accidents will not hurt as much until I blame others only. So I must accept that I have contributed and take the consequence. Most of all, I have to learn from it by studying how it started so I know how to avoid it next time.

20. I believe that if I am delayed by traffic and will be late to an appointment or to work, I must ask, "Is this situation life-threatening?" If not, why should I worry and be upset? There's nothing I can do anyway except increase my blood pressure and maybe ruin my day.

21. As this is an opportunity for me to show kindness and patience where I can use my defensive driving techniques, which will reward me with more than I give, I believe that it is not only my duty but also my responsibility to help and be kind to other drivers if they make a mistake.

22. I believe that when somebody makes a driving mistake that nearly results in an accident, I must help improve the situation through defensive driving and accident avoidance techniques, and I must show no anger, but smile instead. If I do not help, I could suffer physically and financially; thus, I cannot blame anybody but me because I was sleeping on the job.

23. Instead of being angry at other drivers' perceived errors, I believe that I must stretch my helping hand and understand—doing this doesn't plant a bad seed for others to harvest.

24. If I do nothing to help and anticipate a driver's next move because I have the right of way and if an accident happens, I fail miserably because the accident is preventable by me.

25. I believe that even if it is not my fault, if I do not help and I'm in an accident, I will still not feel good. No amount of finger-pointing will elevate my suffering, especially if I am confined in a wheelchair, alive but dead and to be buried a few years later.

26. I believe that I can be in an accident not because I don't know how to drive but because I do not drive defensively, the only way to protect myself regardless of who is at fault and not to shorten my life.

27. I believe that in driving or any aspect in life, if I go through some difficulties or challenges that seem to make life harder to bear and understand, maybe there's a message. I do not despair, but I analyze it, and I know that something positive or a benefit that I can use waits. The situation is not to push me out but to push me up so I stay in faith. This situation is placed to polish me.

28. I believe that I can overcome almost any driver's mistakes; thanks to God for giving me the knowledge and ability to avoid a possible bad situation and turn it into a happy ending by way of defensive driving techniques and also with compassion and understanding.

Chapter 21

Things I Know and Believe about Safe Driving

1. Learning to drive defensively is so compelling because there are too many lives being lost in the roads, too much financial expense wasted, too many productive and healthy individuals maimed, and too many properties destroyed and wasted. When I am well versed in defensive driving and accident avoidance techniques, I can, for sure, help reduce the accidents to a minimum. Plus, I will then make driving more enjoyable and safer, because I not only learn to prevent possible accidents but will also become more courteous, helpful, and forgiving of other road users' perceived shortcomings. I will then easily smile, which

   A. is the most effective way to communicate;

   B. is the most powerful tool to soften anybody's heart;

   C. is the best light switch that turns the lamp on; and

   D. is the best way to show caring, respect, and friendliness.

Note

   a. Blowing of horn and showing the fist or middle-finger hand salute are never right but always wrong as they invite road rage.

b. Most drivers or road users are on my side, not against me, but why do some do things to aggravate or to endanger my life?

c. Learning defensive driving and accident avoidance techniques, one will find out that driving errors are mostly without malice or not done deliberately.

Here are some factors that can contribute to driver's error:

a. New and limited driving experience

b. Looking for addresses or which way to go

c. Distracted or confused by pedestrian or other driver's action

d. Distracted by passengers, loud radio, cell phone use, etc.

e. Driver's view obstructed by signs, shrubs, or vehicle

f. Road condition due to barricades and/or potholes

g. Signs not too visible, nonexistent, or too close to ramp entrance and/or to merging lane

h. Use of drug, prescribed or not, and/or alcohol

i. Drivers that are running from the law

j. Sudden presence of emergency vehicle

k. Avoiding vehicle whose driver is not following traffic rules and regulations

l. Weather condition due to sun glare, rain, snow, fog, and/or slippery road surface

1. I am not making excuses for any driving infractions, but there are many instances and reasons they happen. Remember that those involved are human beings too—subject to human failings due to changing emotions, stresses, decision lapses, environmental challenges, and vehicle failures.

2. If I brighten up when behind the wheel even though I don't feel like smiling, I am telling my body to be happy, and in turn, it responds positively. I don't wait till I feel good to be happy; this is the wrong way. I know fully well that I am responsible for my emotion; this kind of attitude helps me to project a good vibration to my fellow drivers.

3. Having the right of way is no guarantee that I will be safe all the time or not be involved in an accident. I have to be ready to compensate and help for the shortcomings, carelessness, or irresponsible behavior of other drivers.

4. Defensive driving and accident avoidance techniques are common-sense ways to keep my eyes and ears open for the first sign of trouble developing around me. Accidents can happen in a split second, so I need to know and be ready to apply my defensive techniques to prevent a collision.

5. My failure to prevent an accident will not hurt me as much until I blame others. I have to share the blame, the pain, and not spread the anger.

6. My failure to take and apply defensive driving and accident avoidance techniques may take me to where I don't plan to go yet.

7. I should not try to collect debt for the wrong thing a driver has done. I will only get hurt if I expect others to pay me back.

8. If I am in an accident, it is not because I don't know how to drive but because I don't drive defensively.

9. Nobody can take away my joy when I am behind the wheel unless I give it away. I don't focus on the weeds; I can't change them. I ignore so I can bloom.

10. As a true defensive driver, I choose which battle to fight; road rage is not one of them. I just ignore others' negative and destructive behaviors.

11. Green lights give me permission to proceed but do not guarantee that I will be safe. Knowing that my health and life are at stake, I must always check traffic from left to right before I proceed.

12. The government can take my driver's license away for safety reasons, but other drivers are worse; they can take my health and/or life in a split second for no fault of my own.

13. Knowledge of defensive driving and accident avoidance techniques is my only protector to help and guide me as I am alone when behind the wheel.

14. Knowledge of defensive driving and accident avoidance techniques is the gun for a soldier, my life jacket at water or at sea, my talent in life, my air to breathe, my food for nutrients, and my clothing for the weather.

15. After getting my driver's license, it's just the beginning of my driving life. Like after learning to read and write, it is not the end; I must finish high school, college, or university. Some don't even stop here; they go further by taking a master's or doctorate degree for obvious reasons. So after passing the road test, I must take and learn defensive driving and accident avoidance techniques for my safety and driving enjoyment.

16. I would not attempt to climb Mount Everest just because I have climbed a smaller mountain before, without knowing about high-altitude survival techniques and the proper equipment needed. Like if I drive without knowing defensive driving and accident avoidance techniques, it would be suicidal on my part.

17. If others can frustrate me, they are, in fact, controlling my emotion. So I must look past other drivers' weaknesses and look at what I can do to help.

18. When I am behind the wheel, the more I am in a hurry, the quicker I go to the cemetery.

19. Winners are those that help, never those that do not care to compensate for the careless and irresponsible behavior of others, which endanger responsible drivers.

20. If other drivers look at me from the outside, I look at them from the heart, because I can't waste my energy, fighting things that are insignificant.

21. If I make a driving error, I don't expect other drivers to cheer me up, so if they show some negative behavior or displeasure, I ignore it, just smile, accept it, and learn from it.

22. One second of patience for a safe and enjoyable driving experience is all I need to prevent a lifetime of regret.

23. Mistakes committed by other drivers are not intended to give me a hard time but a challenge on my defensive skill to apply, notice, and prevent possible accidents.

24. By having an attitude like the "king of the road" drivers who deliberately behave with contempt toward their fellow drivers increase the risk of traffic accidents.

25. I should not shut love from my fellow drivers out of my daily driving experiences. I must continue to prevent accidents and be courteous as long as I still have something to give, because nothing is over until I stop being behind the wheel.

26. The quickest way to get driving cooperation and feel safe is to give the same; however, the fastest way to lose harmony in the road is to deny reciprocity of others' positive behavior.

27. Driving is a journey for everyone to enjoy every mile of the way, so I must not run my driving life so fast that I forget the safety of all.

28. Delays that happen, I believe, are designed for me to escape from negative things that might happen or are tests of my ability to accept the inevitable.

29. Defensive driving is the mother of all safe driving techniques; it helps to share safety and do what other drivers cannot do for themselves.

30. It may not be my fault for being in a driving accident, but it can be my fault for not accepting part of the blame and not learning from it.

31. I must get an alternate way to bring myself home if there's no designated driver whenever I had more fun from a party than what the law allows.

32. I should not fight a traffic jam but use it to refine my driving and be more accepting of situations that are beyond my control. Anger will only impair all my driving skills and behaviors. Traffic challenges will come to pass as they are only temporary.

33. Some young drivers spend their youth driving crazily and then spend their old age nursing their aches and pains, for drivers who only look for their present pleasure are certain to miss the good things their future brings.

34. I can't expect other drivers to always drive the way I want them to. I can be old but still have not educated them all. Thus, I should minimize and help rectify what other drivers miss to do. Even good drivers are also human and can make mistakes too.

35. To be a responsible driver, it is not how I can make life miserable for other drivers but what I can do to help and make life better for everyone, by not

    A. blowing my horn if others make a mistake;

    B. passing too close to the other vehicle to show my displeasure; or

    C. being discourteous and/or showing my middle-finger hand salute.

36. Most drivers are on my side, not against me, but why do they sometimes do things that can endanger me?

    a. It can be due to lack of driving experience.

    b. It can be due to any of the following:

        1. Looking for an address

        2. Road or weather conditions

        3. Passenger distraction

4.   The sun blinding the driver's eyes

5.   Loud music and/or cell phone use

6.   Driver's physical and mental conditions

37.   The best test of a good driver is how he or she can avoid/solve a possible collision regardless of who is at fault, thus the need to learn defensive driving and accident avoidance techniques. Consider the following:

a.   In any sport, could be just a hobby or professional, when one learns to shoot the basketball through the ring, learns to use the bat and run to the bases in baseball, learns to hit the golf ball, or learns to box, does he stop to learn and expect to be a better player and achieve the desired goal he has dreamed of?

b.   Knowing that there's very keen competition in any sport activity, if I don't have a coach or a trainer and stop learning to improve my skills, what chance do I have to keep abreast with the other players?

c.   What chance do I have to compete against the "Iron Chef" without professional training or at least reading books on cooking and lots of practice, if I learn to cook from my parents or friends only?

d.   It is a very slow process and expensive way to learn anything by just having more practice without professional help. It is cheaper and quicker to learn from the professionals directly or, at least, to read books to acquire the tested experiences. If I limit myself from learning the newer and better ways to do things, thinking that I have learned everything I need to know, it is just false pride. I believe that no one knows all the tricks of the trade from the start.

e.   Could I go to the Olympic Games without rigorous training for many years? No way. But let us assume I am accepted. The best thing that will happen to me is that I will not get any medal for excellence.

f.   In driving, I can be lucky to survive my driving life with only some traffic tickets, small scratches and dents, increased insurance premiums, and loss of valuable time in attending to traffic problems.

38. When I see confusion or accidents in the roads, it depresses me, but if I never do anything to help alleviate the situation, it does not matter how much I sympathize with the victims if I do not take or read on defensive driving; sympathy helps no one.

    a. Thus, I don't wait to get started, give excuses, or put off learning defensive driving and accident avoidance techniques. There's no better time than now to improve the enjoyment and safety when I am behind the wheel. Intentions and promises don't count.

    b. One thing I noticed when I took defensive driving and accident avoidance techniques is that most, if not all, of the annoying habits or behaviors of some drivers or other road users seemed to have disappeared.

    c. Many drivers feel helpless, thinking that there are too many problems in the road—*I'm just one driver.* Don't forget that we are created to do our share to help better this world, and every little thing adds up, for we have something unique to contribute.

39. I don't listen to those that say that I don't need defensive driving. I ignore them because I love to live and value my life. I expect other drivers to make mistakes; it's human nature. Knowing defensive driving, I can see and observe early those situations that can develop into vehicle conflict, so I can help and do something to abort the collision regardless of who is at fault.

40. The basic tool for success for every driver is driving defensively through the early indoctrination of defensive driving and accident avoidance techniques. It provides the necessary skills to fix their attention not only on their right of way but also on what they can do to help prevent a possible vehicle conflict, having the last clear chance.

41. I should be a now person that doesn't procrastinate, not one that says, "One day I will take defensive driving and accident avoidance techniques" but never does. If I make excuses to justify the delay, saying, next week, then next month to next year until it's too late.

42. Nothing is more important in driving than learning defensive driving and accident avoidance techniques, for my safety depends on it. Every driver should not be allowed to drive indefinitely without learning defensive driving or having passed tests on defensive driving for everyone's safety.

43. In driving, it is very seldom that only one driver makes the driving error; more often than not, other drivers contribute to it by not recognizing a developing driving conflict. Sometimes they see it but refuse to help because it is their right of way—what kind of mentality is that? Will they not appreciate also if somebody helps them if they make a mistake?

45. Self-preservation should be paramount. Nobody should be hurt, maimed, in a wheelchair, bedridden, and/or suffering from arthritis pain for the rest of one's life. This is no fun to live, and no amount of blaming other people will bring back the health one used to have.

CHAPTER 22

To Be a Defensive and Safe Driver

1. Whether I have an accident-free driving record or not, I must still read books on defensive driving.

2. I must realize that I can never absorb or retain all that I have learned or read about the different defensive driving techniques. I need a book to refresh me from time to time—my nourishment for survival.

3. I have to accept that just like anything I do in life, things change for the better. If I do not keep myself abreast of the newer and better ways to drive safely, I could be left in the dark.

4. I believe that to learn traffic laws and defensive driving techniques through accidents is a more expensive proposition because it hurts physically and financially.

5. I need to refresh my knowledge on traffic laws, regulations, and defensive driving the moment I do not enjoy driving that much or other drivers are getting to my nerves.

6. I should not wait for the government or insurance company to tell me that I need to take a defensive driving course or review the traffic laws and regulations because of traffic infractions or accidents; it would be rather late and expensive.

7. If I am in an accident or nearly have one, I study to find out what I could have done in order not to repeat the same predicament. I do not

dwell on the other driver's shortcomings because I can't do anything. I have to study what happens and know the defense.

8. I should realize that accidents will not hurt me that much until I blame others only, because I must have contributed to it. Either not seeing it prior to the accident did not help avoid it, or it's because of lack of skill on defensive driving and accident avoidance techniques.

9. I believe that the advantage of knowing defensive driving and accident avoidance techniques is necessary to all drivers. As an agent of change, one has to spread the good news to everyone. Attend a class or have a book on the above subject matter as a bathroom reading material and a handy reference.

10. I must also know that no matter how good a defensive driver I am, if the vehicle I drive is not mechanically sound, I can still have an accident and be guilty of negligence.

11. I believe that every driver must act like a babysitter; they do not wait for the baby to be in trouble before they do something. Knowing that I am judged by my ability to help avoid traffic accidents, the knowledge of defensive driving and accident avoidance techniques is the best solution.

CHAPTER 23

To Be a Part of the Solution and for the Safety of Road Users

1. I happen to know and believe that health is not everything, but when it is lost, I lose everything. Also, I believe that the length of driving experience or education I have does not define a driver; defensive driving and accident avoidance techniques do.

2. After I learned defensive driving and accident avoidance techniques, I felt very fortunate and blessed that I understand road challenges better and am able to help solve traffic challenges that confront me. Thus, I believe that to drive safely and to enjoy every moment of it, everyone does their share by learning defensive driving, and it will make driving safer and more enjoyable.

3. Just like after I finish my schooling, to help me better prepare for my profession and hobby, I take special courses in order to intelligently solve my daily challenges, but if I don't, it might only hamper my advancement. But not in driving—accidents can do more harm to my health and life. So when it comes to learning defensive driving and accident avoidance techniques, I should take the same enthusiasm, knowing that limiting or not taking advantage of the experiences of drivers that were ahead of me is suicidal. I will not go to war without intensive combat training first. Knowing how to shoot a gun is just one important aspect of survival.

4. Even though I do not have as many years of driving experience as others, with the knowledge of defensive driving and accident avoidance

techniques, I can honestly say that I will have the ability to turn possible vehicular conflict to a safer conclusion.

5. Even though I cannot completely eliminate all traffic accidents, if I can help reduce the number of lives being lost; lessen property damage; reduce the amount spent for lawyer's fees; lower insurance premiums; and prevent wasting productive time, loss of breadwinners, and loss of dependents' bright future, it would be a good start.

6. After I learn defensive driving and accident avoidance techniques, I found out that

   a. there are times when drivers fail to follow traffic rules and regulations for whatever reason;

   b. there are times when drivers are not always physically and/or mentally fit to drive;

   c. sometimes pedestrians don't follow safety rules and are hidden from the driver's view;

   d. there are times when roads and weather conditions are not ideal for driving; and

   e. there are times when vehicles driven are not mechanically in good working conditions.

Note

   a. I strongly believe that defensive driving is the best solution against any of the above.

7. I must accept that in my past driving experiences, I made mistakes too. Thanks to other drivers' defensive driving skills, they prevented a possible collision. Although I was lucky, I cannot depend on others to keep protecting me; I must do my part. The lack of knowledge and practice of defensive driving makes me an average and unsafe driver.

8. I know for a fact that lots of drivers take special courses to prepare for the jobs they are applying for or to be able to better solve the challenges they encounter in their professions. But there's no denying that some do

not have the same enthusiasm to learn defensive driving, not realizing that collisions can do more harm to an individual. Defensive driving and accident avoidance techniques provide knowledge to predict, analyze, and/or anticipate situations that can lead to vehicle conflict, not to mention the ability to better control emotions when behind the wheel.

9. If I cannot add more years to my driving life, at least I should add more enjoyment and safety to whatever is left of my driving days. I believe that every driver is the architect of his or her own enjoyment, safety, and/or health.

10. Some drivers make the roads their racetracks, which, of course, helps the towing and body shops, mortuaries, and hospitals to flourish but at one's own risk, causing traffic jams and hindering the police from doing their primary job—that is, to protect the citizens. Driving journey is measured best by the number of collisions he or she can help and prevent, never the number of vehicles that had eaten their dust.

11. In driving, I cannot be too sure of my safety; there's always the first time, or worse, it could be the last time or too late to rectify what has happened. So before this happens, I learn defensive driving and accident avoidance techniques to have a better chance of protecting my health and life.

12. I believe that a driver that has learned defensive driving and accident avoidance techniques may live to drive another day. I know that drivers doing nothing to better prepare themselves and their family may find out sooner or later that there will be collateral damage that cannot be reversed.

13. I believe that if I haven't learned defensive driving and accident avoidance techniques and the application, I will be considered a selfish or unconcerned individual. However, if I consider myself responsible, but the moment I settle for less than what I deserve, I will be sorry if I get what I didn't wish for.

14. I believe that there's no such thing as a safe driver that can protect other road users and himself without the knowledge and practice of defensive driving and accident avoidance techniques. Also, one thing I have

noticed about learning defensive driving is that all the annoying habits and behaviors of drivers seem to have disappeared.

15. In the roads sometimes it is every man for himself. Having the knowledge of defensive driving and accident avoidance techniques, I am ready in a split second to prevent a possible collision—my advantage—because without it, I will not have the necessary tools to help others and be safe myself.

16. I believe that everything has a beginning and an end; learning defensive driving and accident avoidance techniques should be the beginning, and the end is the application and being a courteous and a helpful driver regardless of who has the right of way.

17. I believe that every driver doesn't always drive properly or drive safely, but he must be forgiven and helped, thus the origin of defensive driving and accident avoidance techniques. Because nobody can claim that they drive without a mistake.

18. I believe that we should not be too busy as to delay learning defensive driving, because challenges in the roads will never be eliminated; ignoring the reality might be too late and be very expensive indeed. Wait no more, get started, and don't keep putting it off.

19. I believe that if a survey is made on all vehicle collisions, half have the right of way, and the other half don't, but even the ones that have the right of way cannot escape physical injury or even death. This necessitates the need to take defensive driving seriously, and the earlier the better. Prevention is always better than the cure.

20. I believe that with all the campaign about the benefits of defensive driving, why on earth would I be driving not knowing the best protection in the road? Defensive driving and accident avoidance techniques save thousands of dollars, man-hours, frustrations, and/or aggravations, but the most important reasons are my health and life.

21. I believe that to have road safety, I must first have knowledge on defensive driving. I should not reject wisdom; only foolish people do. I must, instead, beg to acquire and possess the skills for the safety and protection of all road users including me.

22. I believe that knowledge of defensive driving provides me the knowledge of a driver with twenty or more years of driving experience even if I'm a new driver. I too believe that drivers that don't possess knowledge on defensive driving techniques learn it slowly or by having accidents, which can be costly. A safe driver is not that expensive, but a cheap driver is more costly and more dangerous to one's life and health.

23. I believe that I can't be like other drivers who only do something after having an accident or traffic ticket and/or when insurance gets too expensive for the pocketbook. Defensive driving is akin to a parachute or life jacket when it comes to driving.

24. I know that in the course of my driving life, it will never run smoothly all the time, so I must be ready for any eventuality. Because even in an ideal driving condition, only the ones trained in defensive driving and accident avoidance techniques have a better skill of helping and avoiding possible collisions.

25. I know that even if I could handle my vehicle well, but if I'm not well versed on defensive driving and accident avoidance techniques, conflict with other road users is still inevitable. I would not have the knowledge to foretell and the defense to situations that can lead to vehicle conflict.

26. I know that if I want to be safe on the roads but I don't study the principles of accident avoidance techniques, I would be driving blindly and not safe. Knowing that safety does not come to me, I have to study defensive driving because there's more to driving than just turning and stopping.

27. I know that miserable drivers love company, so I must be on guard; otherwise, I will be a recruit. As a result, I will experience stress in my daily driving unless I'm knowledgeable on defensive driving techniques. It is not even mandatory, but highly recommended to all drivers.

28. I know that driving is like a lottery; I can only win if I buy a ticket. Likewise in driving, I will have the chance to prevent any possible accident if I have taken defensive driving, because I can recognize potential accidents early and apply accident avoidance techniques.

29. I know that self-preservation is the first law of nature, so I shouldn't delay studying defensive driving and accident avoidance techniques to

prepare me for the unexpected, because nothing is certain in driving. If not, I'll be doomed to suffer the consequence.

30. I know that when I have a near-accident and am helped by other drivers to dodge it, I consider it to be my lucky day, but I can't depend on others' generosity all the time, those that take the extra mile to help me. I have to learn defensive driving for my own safety and to do my share to willingly spread safety in the road.

31. I know that passing the driving test is only the beginning of my driving life. The next thing for me is to learn defensive driving and accident avoidance techniques to survive and be able to help other drivers when needed. Even small or near-accidents, sooner or later, will escalate to an occasion where my loved ones and I will regret, as accidents are dreadful occurrences, so I must be ready at any moment to avoid it.

32. I know that I must have the knowledge of how to practice defensive driving and accident avoidance techniques early in my driving because it's my life jacket or lifeline—a must so I can prevent lots of frustrations, headaches, regrets, and blame later.

33. I know that I cannot be a true defensive driver without first learning defensive driving and accident avoidance techniques; it will instill in me how to be courteous and helpful. I am also of the belief that once I am a defensive driver, I will always be a defensive driver.

34. I know that I don't know everything about defensive driving at the outset of my driving, so I stay open for any chance to improve my defensive skills, because even a minor improvement or adjustment in my driving ability, for sure, will be a big improvement to road safety.

35. I know that if I make excuses for not having the time to learn defensive driving, I might later regret it, and no amount of blaming others will change what negative situation had happened. So I don't wait for an accident to force me, if I am given a second chance, to learn how to spot possible vehicle conflict—the knowledge on how to help and avoid regardless of who has the right of way.

36. I know that if I have a big ego, thinking that I am a good driver and that an accident cannot happen on my watch, I could be wrong on purpose. I would not only be dangerous to my health and life but also

affect my family, my friends, and all road users. I must be, instead, an asset to humanity, not a liability.

37. I know that learning defensive driving is for my own protection or insurance; to secure against loss, it is an equalizer to anything that confronts me in the road. As long as we have accidents due to traffic, I should keep searching and educating myself for the solutions, which are within my and every driver's capacity. I can't depend on others for my safety as it's within my power to be educated on defensive driving and accident avoidance techniques.

38. I know that I must not use my energy in complaining about other drivers' mistakes or way of driving, but I must use it to study defensive driving techniques; this will make me more accepting to others' mistakes and more calm.

39. I know that if I dream of having a driver's license to enjoy the fun of being behind the wheel, I must also be prepared for the challenges that test my survival, because there's more than just stopping, starting, turning, and/or enjoying the fresh air.

40. I know that not everybody was born to be patient and helpful, let alone be a defensive driver. If I'm left on my own, I will slowly learn the above characteristics, but it will take me a long time or via an accident, which is not the preferred way. I must take defensive driving to shorten my learning curve and prior to an event that I cannot fix or reverse. I must be a part of the driving solution and not a part of the driving problem.

Having no accident should not embolden anyone to delay learning defensive driving and accident avoidance techniques.

CHAPTER 24

What Do I Need to Be a Safe and Responsible Driver?

1. I must possess good driving attitude and knowledge on defensive driving and accident avoidance techniques;

2. I must be knowledgeable of all traffic rules and regulations and driving procedures to help move traffic orderly and safely;

3. I must know that even if someone does something wrong or makes a driving mistake, I may still be held responsible for the collision if I am found to have had the last chance to avoid the accident but didn't do anything to prevent it;

4. I must cooperate, be predictable, be courteous, not cut off anybody, signal when I turn or change lanes, and make sure my signal is off when the maneuver is done;

5. I must give adequate space between the vehicles in my front and back, give enough time for other drivers to finish their maneuver without rushing them, and make myself visible all the time by not being in anyone's blind spot;

6. I must communicate with all road users by my signal—eye contact and hand signal—so pedestrians, cyclists, and riders of motorized wheelchairs will know exactly what to do;

7. I must be aware that the following greatly diminish one's ability to operate a motor vehicle:

    a. Illness

    b. Being emotionally upset

    c. Mental and physical fatigue

    d. Taking illicit drugs and even those prescribed or over-the-counter if abused or if caution is not followed;

8. I must have a headlight that is aimed properly to be able to see at night and in poor-light driving conditions, like in fog, snow, or rain, and to illuminate properly pedestrians, animals, and other vehicles;

9. I must keep checking my blind spot by frequently glancing on my right and left-side outside mirror by turning my head over my shoulder and not letting other drivers stay long there by adjusting my speed;

10. I must be extra careful, observe other drivers' moves, and be ever ready to help if needed regardless of who has the right of way, especially early morning and late afternoon when the sunlight shines directly on drivers' eyes. They may not see traffic signs or have a problem recognizing the color of the traffic lights. Also at dusk and dawn, because drivers are adjusting to the changing light condition;

11. I must look well ahead of my driving lane and watch for road signs, traffic, and pedestrians. I also look for parked vehicles to find out if there's a driver or passenger inside. The driver might open the door or move forward without first checking for traffic behind. Passengers might also exit using the roadside door. At a distance, I check underneath the vehicle to see a sign, like a foot, if there's somebody trying to cross that is shielded by the vehicle. If I can make a lane change, I would, to leave a space cushion between me and the parked vehicles;

12. I must obey maximum posted speed limits; always assess the road, traffic, and/or weather condition; and adjust my speed accordingly;

13. I must be aware that although cruise control improves fuel economy and prevents from going over the speed limit, it will not be wise to use it when the road is slippery, icy, or wet. I may not use it also when traffic is heavy or if I'm tired; it can hypnotize me and make me lose concentration;

14. I must follow police officers' or construction people's direction even though it is different from the traffic sign. I stop as far to the side of the road as possible when stopped by a police officer for the officer's safety and everybody's; and

15. I must always leave a space cushion between me and other vehicles so that I will be able to stop without hitting anybody, especially in an emergency. In bad weather, I give more space cushion especially when I am following a motorcycle and/or commercial trucks.

Note

a. For me, the true measure of a good driver is the number of times I help avoid and prevent an accident, having the last clear chance, regardless of who is at fault.

CHAPTER 25

What I Do if I'm in the Market
for a New or Used Vehicle

1. First, to know my score, I get my credit report and make sure the entries are correct. This is to avoid lowering my score by the multiple checking of the different companies and to save the fee they charge.

2. I search for the best financing among banks, the dealers, and other institutions to know their rate and what I can qualify for. I also research on the most suitable vehicle that meets my needs and is within my capacity to pay.

3. I must also evaluate and decide whether I will keep my old vehicle or buy a new or used vehicle and research on the advantages and disadvantages between buying and leasing.

4. If I am considering selling my old vehicle on my own, I must know the book value and what competitors are asking and be prepared for the inconveniences and the hassles of dealing with strangers and missed appointments.

5. For a better price, less pressure, and more convenience, once I have decided to buy a new vehicle, I do my research online. For fine prints and return policy, I have the dealer to explain and have all spoken promises to be in writing and initialed to be enforceable.

6. I also check different insurance companies, their consumer reports, rates, deductibles, discounts for low annual mileage and safe driver, and discounts if vehicle, home, and/or apartment are insured together.

7. I must not order any accessories from the dealer if I can get it cheaper elsewhere. I have the vehicle inspected by an independent mechanic, even a slightly used vehicle.

8. I also get the dealers to compete with each other. I do the bidding process by phone or even by e-mail to save time and for less pressure. I do this after I have decided the make, style, and model of the vehicle I want to buy. I deal only with the manager of the dealership; they are the only ones that can make the decision outside their normal business practice.

Note

a. I sign the contract only after reading it carefully. Any ambiguous word must be explained and rewritten in laymen's language before I sign the dotted line.

b. I don't take delivery or possession of the vehicle before all the things to be done are completed and approved by me as previously agreed.

c. Before I ask a relative or a friend to cosign if my credit or income is below what is required to buy or lease a vehicle, I have to make sure I'll be able to meet my obligation. Otherwise, I will create an enemy for life and lose their confidence and future help.

d. Likewise, if I'm not ready and willing to take the responsibility in case they default, because I am equally responsible for the loan, I should not cosign for somebody and have sleepless nights.

CHAPTER 26

What I Do if There's an Emergency Vehicle with Siren and Flashing Lights On

I yield the right of way to all emergency vehicles when their lights are flashing and the siren is on, like ambulance, police, or fire trucks that are nearby, responding to an alarm. They can be coming from any direction. As a defensive driver,

1. I right away check traffic on my right side, I signal when safe, and then I pull to the right curb on a two-way street or to the left or right curb on a one-way road, whichever is closer, but always clear of any intersection so as not to block traffic;

2. I would drive as close as possible to the curb and remain stopped until the emergency vehicle or vehicles have passed unless, of course, directed by a police officer;

3. I check traffic behind, signal, and double-check for safety before I move forward to make sure I am safe from all emergency vehicles and/or traffic as drivers tend to get erratic; and

4. I must never drive or follow close to any emergency vehicle as they sometimes do some correction of their direction and not to add confusion; besides, it is against the law.

Note

a.   I must have my radio or conversation on a low volume so as not to be distracted and miss hearing the siren or seeing the emergency flashing lights.

CHAPTER 27

What I Have Learned about Mobile Phone Use While Driving

1. It distracts me, the driver, and has been proven to have caused the increasing number of accidents; thus, many governments' jurisdictions have passed a law that makes it illegal to use the cell phone while driving.

2. It is similar to that associated with other distractions; it increases crash risk, according to the American National Highway Traffic Safety Administration (NHTSA).

3. It causes me, the driver, to be inattentive to the driving task, which is a big factor for all reported traffic crashes.

Note

a. If I have to make a call, so as not to risk having an accident (this applies to hands-free telephones as well), I pull over to the side of the road in a safe place to stop.

CHAPTER 28

What Must I Do Before Any Maneuver?

I do the following:

    a.   Check my inside mirror.

    b.   Check the outside mirror, left or right.

    c.   Check my blind spot, left or right.

    d.   Signal my intention, left or right.

Note

    a.   If the first three above are not favorable, I repeat the process.

    b.   I signal only when the first three above are okay to tell others of my intention.

    c.   I execute the maneuver, but I keep checking for safety.

For every driver's mistake due to unfavorable weather or road conditions, the one trained in defensive driving and accident avoidance techniques usually has the ability to avoid or lessen the severity of an accident regardless of who has the right of way.

Backing is dangerous, but accidents can be easily prevented if done properly:

a. First I go around the vehicle to check for hazards before I get inside my vehicle.

b. I take the proper backing position once inside so as not to strain my neck and for better view.

c. I back up slowly while checking for pedestrians and vehicles behind.

d. If a pedestrian or a vehicle is approaching, I stop; they have the right of way.

Note

a. If proper backing position is not taken, the driver's view at the back will be limited.

b. Depending only on the inside and outside mirrors for backing will not give a complete view of the back—very unsafe.

c. Even though the back is clear, I stop, check, and move slowly.

d. If my view is blocked by a vehicle or anything, I move slowly. If there's a passenger, I ask them to check outside.

e. If possible, I back up to park or go forward to the next stall if vacant.

f. Preferably, I park far from buildings for physical exercise and less traffic and hassle.

g. Driving between parked vehicles, I look for white backup lights or smoke from the tailpipe, and I warn the driver by tapping my horn and proceed only when safe.

h. I make sure my backup light is working to help drivers and pedestrians know if I'm backing.

In conclusion, I help avoid an accident, regardless of who is at fault or has the right of way, for less hassle. It takes only a second or two versus hours attending to matters related to the accident; I don't compromise my health or life. How can I go wrong if I extend a helping hand? Besides, it gives me a nice feeling being able to help.

CHAPTER 29

Why I Learn Defensive Driving and Accident Avoidance Techniques

1. That if I drive aggressively, not only is it very dangerous to all road users, not appreciated, and never an indication of my skill, but is also rather my ignorance, lack of consideration to others, and show-off attitude.

2. That if I drive fast or overestimate my ability to stop on time, I will pay the price of hitting the vehicle ahead if they have to stop suddenly.

3. That I should not be drawn to battles that do not matter. As a driver, I choose which battle to engage in, and road rage is not one of them. What I do is, I just ignore negative behaviors because I can never win, only waste time and court more trouble. Besides, I am an eagle; I don't fight crows.

4. That if I make a driving mistake, I should not expect other road users to cheer me up. I accept and ignore if they show me negative gestures or behaviors. I have to accept my mistake and give a sign of apology.

5. That if other drivers look at me from the outside when I make a driving mistake, I look at them from the heart, because I know some like to find fault to make them look smarter and a better driver.

6. That I must take or read on defensive driving and accident avoidance techniques so I have something to use and apply to help keep me protected when I am behind the wheel as there are all kinds of

challenges from drivers, other road users, the weather, and road conditions.

7. That if I do not take or read on defensive driving, it would be like having no life vest when I go fishing or sailing in the lake or ocean. Defensive driving gives me a fighting chance of surviving in case something happens to endanger my life regardless of who is at fault. I must help if I have the last clear chance to prevent an accident, because driving is helping one another. Everybody is entitled to make a mistake without malice.

8. That if I stop educating myself as soon as I can read or write, I will be curtailing my progress in life, and I have to take further education because higher education is known to provide better qualification, better pay, and a higher position in a company. In other words, there is a reward for expanding knowledge, but losing life or health is not at stake. Not like in driving—the more I know about defensive driving and accident avoidance techniques, the better chance I can avoid an accident that can cause physical injury, and I can save myself from all kinds of troubles and headaches.

9. That I would not wash windows in a high-rise building, climb a tall tree, or work in a high-rise construction without a lifeline to protect me from getting hurt. That's why I would not drive without having learned defensive driving and accident avoidance techniques to have the knowledge to help avoid and protect me from an accident.

10. That the length of experience a driver has does not define a driver; it is one's knowledge on defensive driving and accident avoidance techniques. It provides knowledge on how to help and avoid an accident regardless of who is at fault or has the right of way but on who has the last clear chance.

11. That knowledge of defensive driving and accident avoidance techniques is every driver's interest. One day it will make sense after an accident; if only one knew how to apply defensive driving, it could have been prevented.

12. That to help minimize traffic accidents, the following have to take their share of responsibility:

a.   All drivers—must follow traffic rules and regulations and willingly help when needed by applying defensive techniques regardless of who has the right of way.

b.   Pedestrians—before crossing, must check and double-check left and right to make sure every lane is safe to cross. Even pedestrians have the right of way; it is their limb and life that are at stake. Pedestrians never win against a moving vehicle.

c.   Engineers—must plan, construct, and repair roads for safety and place signs that are visible from a distance to give early warning to drivers so they can make the necessary move to execute the driving maneuver needed.

d.   Local government must make sure that

1.   tree branches do not cover street names—should be seen from a distance;

2.   at intersections and/or parking lots' entrances, no shrubs or commercial signs block the view of drivers; and

3.   numbers for business addresses and private homes should be large and easy to locate.

Note

a.   A bus stop should be cut into the curb so as not to bother the traffic that is using the outside lane. This happens whenever buses stop to kill time, drop, or pick up passengers. Drivers behind are forced to change lanes, sometimes abruptly, and cause accidents.

b.   After an accident or near-accident, every driver should review what had happened to know what has contributed to it. One should not just blame the other driver or pedestrian but should also ask oneself, "What could I have done to avoid or prevent the accident?" It is the right thing to do.

1001 Ways
to Drive Defensively
(Illustrated Situations)

Situation: 1

    a.   Vehicle *A* has a right signal on (fig. 1) prior to *B* that is trying to exit from a parking lot.

Situation: 2

    a.   Vehicle *A* has the right signal while approaching an uncontrolled intersection (fig. 1).

    b.   B vehicles are either going straight or turning left or right (fig. 2).

Situation: 3

    a.   Vehicle *A* turns left from a three-lane road, controlled or not (fig. 1).

    b.   Vehicle *B* is also making a right turn from the opposite side of the road (fig. 2).

Situation: 4

    a.   Vehicle *A* wants to get into a parking lot and does the checking and signaling, except one thing.

    b.   Vehicles *B* and *C* are following behind, and both slow down just a little bit, like vehicle *A*.

Situation: 5

    a.   Vehicle *A* is in a hurry and wants to pass vehicle *B* (fig. 1) when close to an intersection that is controlled or not.

    B.   *A*'s view to check traffic coming from the left or right side is blocked by *B* (fig. 1).

Situation: 6

    a.   Vehicle *A* stops beside vehicle *B* at an intersection due to a red light.

    b.   Vehicle *A* passes *B* as soon as the light changes to green (fig. 1).

Situation: 7

    b.   Vehicle *A* wants to turn left at a busy intersection that has no green turning arrow (fig. 1).

Situation: 8

    a.   Bus stops on the side of the road to pick up or drop passengers (fig. 1).

    b.   Vehicle *A* is making a right turn in the direction of the bus (fig. 2).

    c.   Vehicle *B* on the middle lane is traveling straight through (fig. 3).

Situation: 9

    a.   Bus stops to drop or pick up passengers (fig. 1).

    b.   Vehicles *A*, *B*, and *C* get stuck behind the bus (fig. 2).

    c.   Vehicle *D* on the middle lane is going straight through (fig. 3).

Situation: 10

    a.   Vehicle *A* is getting close to a freeway entrance while using the outside lane (fig. 1).

Situation: 11

    a.   Vehicle *A* is traveling from the middle lane (fig. 1).

    b.   Vehicle *B* and *C* stop at an intersection that is not controlled by traffic lights (fig. 2).

Situation: 12

a. Vehicle *A* is turning left at an intersection controlled with lights but has no green turning arrows, and turning lanes are not in line (fig. 1).

Situation: 13

a. Vehicle *A* is driving in the middle lane (fig. 1).
b. Vehicles are allowed to park on the outside lane of the road (fig. 2).

Situation: 14

a. Vehicle *A* is parked at the top of a T intersection (fig. 1).

Situation: 15

a. Vehicle *A*, truck or van, is parked at the corner entrance of a parking stall (fig. 1).

Situation: 16

a. Vehicle *A* just crossed an intersection that is controlled or not but stops soon after the pedestrian crosswalk due to stop-and-go traffic conditions ahead (fig. 1).
b. Vehicle *B* following behind stops before clearing the intersection (fig. 2).

Situation: 17

a. Vehicle *A*, a van or bigger, is parked close to an intersection (fig. 1).

Situation: 18

a. At intersections or parking lots, hedges or commercial signs are blocking the view of drivers to check traffic for safety (fig. 1).

Situation: 19

a. Vehicle *A*, on a green light, moves forward to the middle of the intersection for a left turn, where there's no turning arrow, and following behind is vehicle *B* (fig. 1).

Situation: 20

    a.   Vehicle *A* is turning right at an intersection with red lights (fig. 1).

    b.   With left turning arrow, vehicle *B* is turning left from the opposite side (fig. 2).

Situation: 21

    a.   Vehicle *A* wants to turn left at an intersection that has no traffic lights.

Situation: 22

    a.   Due to a red light, vehicle *A* stops at an intersection (fig. 1).

Situation: 23

    a.   Green lights give vehicle *B* the right to go through an intersection (fig. 1).

Situation: 24

    a.   After shopping, a driver is backing out from a shopping center's parking lot (fig. 1).

Situation: 25

    a.   Driver *A* is driving between parked vehicles in a busy parking lot.

1001 Ways
to Drive Defensively
(Illustrated Situations)

Here are some driving situations and how I apply my defensive driving and accident avoidance techniques. It is up to you—you can read it for pleasure only, or it may enrich your defensive driving and accident avoidance techniques regardless of who is at fault. You decide.

1. Situation

    a. Vehicle A has a right signal on (Fig. 1 next page) prior to vehicle B that is trying to exit from a parking lot.

Danger

    a. Vehicle B can conclude that A is going to turn into the parking lot where B is.

    b. Accident can happen, if B moves forward & A didn't turn into the lot. (Fig. 2)

My defensive techniques in this situation:

    a. I will not put my right signal before B because it can be misinterpreted that I'm turning to the parking lot.

---

b. If I'm B, I must wait for more indications that vehicle A is really turning to the parking lot, before I move forward, like:

1. Is the vehicle slowing down?

2. Is the driver checking the parking lot?

3. Are the front wheels starting to turn right?

c. If all three above are observed, only then will I move forward.

d. Vehicle A should only activate signal when in front of B, not before.

Note

a. Why do drivers have their signal too early or none at all, which confuses others? They change lanes, forget to cancel signal, or worse, those that have no courtesy, Don't signal their intentions at all.

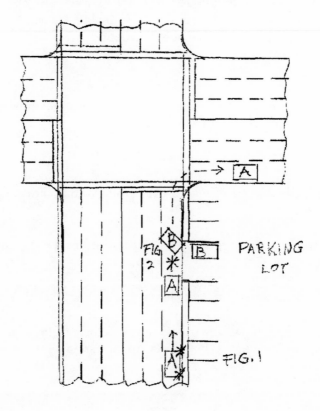

2. Situation

    a. Vehicle A has the right signal while approaching an uncontrolled intersection (Fig. 1 next page A).

    b. B, Vehicles' are either going straight, turn left or right (Fig. 2 next page B).

Danger

    a. Right signal of vehicle A makes B drivers assume that A is turning right.

    b. If any B vehicle either to go straight, left or right turn and A didn't turn at the intersection, but drove straight, a collision will happen. (Fig. 3)

My defensive technique, if I'm any of the B vehicles, before I move, I must see that:

    A. vehicle A is slowing down,

    B. the driver is checking for a right turn, and

    C. the front tires have started to turn right.

Note

    a. Signals do not always indicate what a driver is planning to do—they may have the wrong signal, forget to cancel, or signal early or not at all.

    b. Drivers have to signal to indicate intentions to turn left, right or change lanes—not early, late—and cancel it if it does not come off automatically.

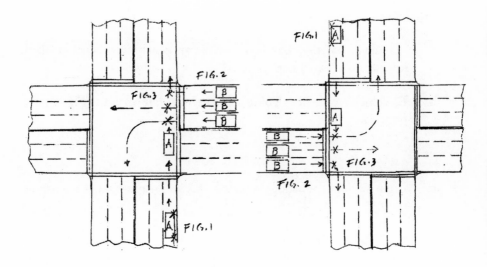

3.   Situation

   a.   Vehicle A is turning left from a three-lane road, controlled or not (Fig. 1 next page A).

   b.   Vehicle B is also making a right turn from the opposite side of the road (Fig. 2 next page B).

Danger

   a.   An accident with B will happen if vehicle A takes the middle lane (Fig. 3).

   b.   An accident with A will happen if B turns at the same time and turns wide (Fig. 3).

My defensive techniques in this situation:

   a.   If I drive vehicle A and turn left from the inside lane (Fig. 1), I must take the same lane then change lanes later if needed (Fig. 4).

   b.   If I am vehicle B, before turning right (Fig. 2), I'll wait and watch A to know which lane they're taking; they could turn wide. I must also check pedestrians that might cross my path from right to left. (Fig. 5 & 6).

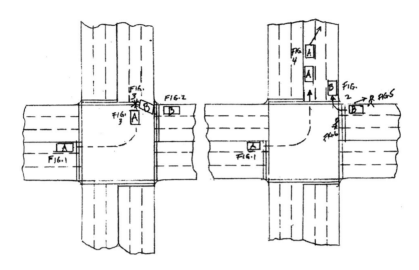

4. Situation

    a. Vehicle A wants to get into a parking lot did the checking & signaling, except one.

    b. Vehicles B & C are following behind, both slowed down just a little bit, like vehicle A.

Danger

    a. Vehicle A can't proceed to turn and has to stop hard; there's a pedestrian on the sidewalk (Fig. 1 next page).

    b. Vehicle B crashes into A, and C does the same to B; both assumed that A can make the turn and were not prepared to stop (Fig. 2 and 3 next page).

My defensive driving techniques in this situation:

    a. Vehicle A should have checked the sidewalk for the presence of pedestrians' or anything that can interfere with the turn, soon after the preparation for the turn (Fig. 4).

b. If I'm B or C, as soon as I notice that A is preparing to turn into the parking lot, I check the sidewalk for possible problems that might force A to stop. (Fig. 4).

Note

a. Sooner or later, the delay to learn defensive driving will be paid for.

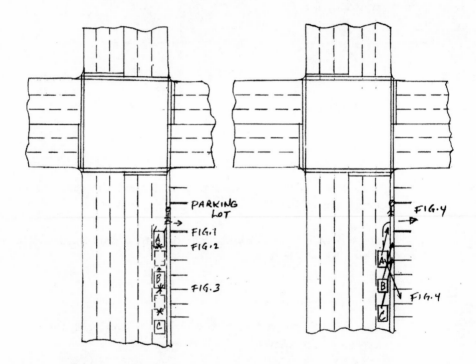

5. Situation

a. Vehicle A is in a hurry and wants to pass vehicle B (Fig. 1 next page) when close to an intersection that is controlled or not.

b. A's view to check traffic coming from the left or right side is blocked by B (Fig. 1).

Danger

a. Passing B close to an intersection by vehicle A, not knowing the traffic condition ahead, is illegal; very dangerous and suicidal (Fig. 2).

My defensive techniques in this situation:

    a.   Even though I'm in a hurry, I would never pass or change lanes at intersections; it confuses other drivers, is illegal, dangerous, suicidal, and against defensive driving.

    b.   Vehicle A will gain no time advantage, but one mistake is all that is needed to end life or health, a prize too high to take (Fig. 2).

Note

    a.   Safety belongs to those who learn defensive driving.

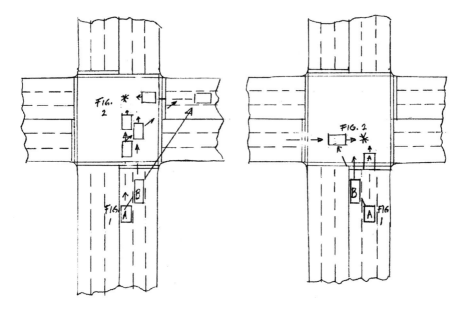

6.   Situation

    a.   Vehicle A stop beside vehicle B at an intersection due to a red light. (see next page)

    b.   Vehicle A tried to pass B as soon as the light changed to green (Fig. 1).

Danger

a. Vehicle A can't see traffic from either situations, B is blocking view of A (Fig. 1).

My defensive technique in this situation:

a. It's against the law and dangerous (Fig. 2) to pass at intersections, it's were traffic crosses its others' path, worst if view to check traffic is covered. (Fig.3)

Note

a. There is no such thing as a safe driver who has not learned defensive driving.

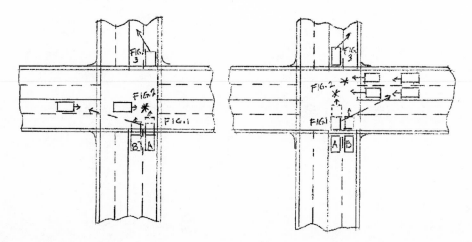

7. Situation

a. Vehicle A wants to turn left at a busy intersection that has no green turning arrow (Fig. 1 next two pages).

Danger

Problems that A will encounter:

    a.   Without turning arrow and if turning bays or lanes are not in line, A will not see traffic from the other side; vehicle B blocks the view of A (Fig. 2).

    b.   If vehicle A turns left blindly on green or when the light turns yellow and the opposite traffic speeds up to race the lights, a head-on collision can happen (Fig. 3).

My defensive techniques in this situation:

A.   Instead of turning left at intersections where there's no turning arrow,

    1.   I change lanes to the outside lane in preparation for right turns (Fig. 4).

    2.   I pass the intersection and make three quick right turns (Fig. 5).

Note

    a.   Learn defensive driving to compensate for the carelessness of other drivers.

    b.   Turning bays should be in line to eliminate blind spots, if there are no turning left arrows.

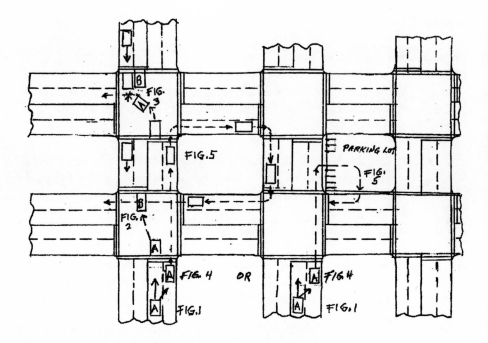

8. Situation

    a. Bus stops on the side of the road to pick up or drop passengers (Fig. 1 next page).

    b. Vehicle A is making a right turn in the direction of the bus (Fig. 2).

    c. Vehicle B on the middle lane is travelling straight through (Fig. 3).

Danger

What can happen if vehicle

    a. A makes a quick lane change upon seeing the bus without checking behind for safety? (Fig. 4)

    b. B doesn't help or anticipate A's predicaments, thinking that it's his right of way? (Fig. 4)

Result

    a.   Collision is inevitable if drivers don't cooperate or anticipate other drivers' challenges, like at a dance floors dancers help and evade possible collision.

My defensive techniques in this situation:

    a.   If I'm vehicle A, I don't lane change suddenly, without checking first for safety. (Fig. 4).

    b.   If I'm vehicle B, regardless of who has the right of way, I anticipate others' moves that can contribute to an accident; I get ready for the defense by slowing down, check traffic behind & cover my brake (Fig. 4).

Note

    a.   By refusing to help avoid accidents, I could get hurt; it takes only a second or two versus hours attending to matters related to the accident.

    b.   To better use police officer's time and to contain the increase of insurance premiums, the destruction of properties, and the safety of the driving public, a bus cutoff should be constructed where roads are busy. (Fig. 5).

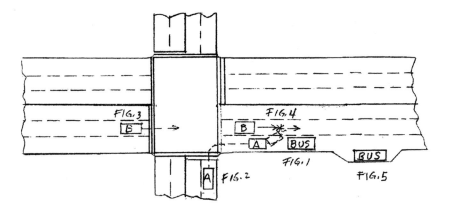

9.   Situation

   a.   Bus stops to drop or pick up passengers (Fig. 1 next page).

   b.   Vehicles A, B, and C get stuck behind the bus (Fig. 2).

   c.   Vehicle D, on the middle lane, is going straight through. (Fig. 3).

Danger

   a.   Bus is blocking lane, vehicles behind have to make a lane change, some without regard to safety.

   b.   Vehicle D may not realize the danger ahead or doesn't care; it's his right of way (Fig. 3).

Result

   a.   An accident can happen if A, B, and C, (Fig. 4) is in a hurry to change lane without first checking for safety.

My defensive techniques in this situation:

   a.   I have to be very careful before making a lane change, if I'm vehicle A, B, or C, knowing that other vehicles in my lane will be trying to do the same. (Fig. 2)

   b.   Vehicle D (Fig. 3) may not realize the danger facing A, B, and C or will not help, since it has the right of way, so the onus is on the vehicles behind the bus to make sure they change lane safely.

Recommendation

   a.   Have a bus cutoff lane (Fig. 5).

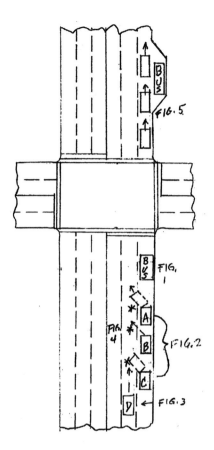

10. Situation

    a.   Vehicle A is getting close to a freeway entrance while using the outside lane (Fig. 1 next page).

Danger

    a.   Competing for the same lane with traffic entering the freeway is not very safe (Fig. 2).

Result

    a.   Drivers that don't apply defensive driving techniques, even those already in the freeway & have the right of way are asking for trouble. (Fig. 3).

My defensive techniques in this situation:

a. If I'm A, I make the outside lane available for traffic entering the freeway, as much as possible.

b. I cooperate with traffic entering the freeway, if I'm stuck in the outside lane I don't insist on my right of way, knowing that I can never be sure about safety when two lanes merge into one.

Note

a. Defensive drivers always select the safest lane to use for maximum safety (Fig. 3)

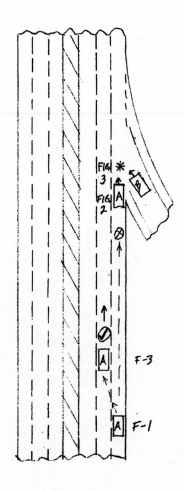

11. Situation

    a.   Vehicle A is using the middle lane (Fig. 1 next page).

    b.   Vehicle B & C stops at an intersection that is not controlled by traffic lights (Fig. 2).

Danger

    a.   If no pedestrians are noticed, driver A may not take precautions, but what if there are pedestrians crossing that are hidden? (Fig. 3)

    b.   Vehicles B and C also blocks A's view to check traffic from the intersection (Fig. 4).

My defensive techniques in this situation if I'm vehicle A:

    a.   I prepare for the worst, somebody might be crossing. If there is nobody, I lose a second not hours, if I have an accident.

    b.   Half a block away (Fig. 1), I ease up on my gas pedal, check traffic behind, slow down, cover my brake, then continue checking for pedestrians ahead.

    c.   Next, still with slow speed, I check traffic at the intersection from left to right, before crossing.

Note

    a.   Pedestrians check vacant lanes; don't assume that if a vehicle had stopped, you are already safe, don't depend on right of way; you can't win in a vehicle collision.

    b.   Drivers must be ready for the defense whenever view is obstructed by a stopped or parked vehicle, commercial signs, bushes or anything that can limit sight Inspection.

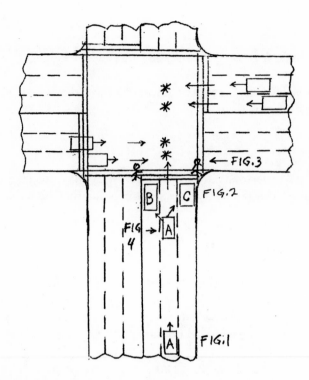

12. Situation

    a.   Vehicle A is turning left at an intersection controlled with lights, but has no green turning arrows and turning lanes are not in line (Fig. 1 next page).

Danger

    a.   Driver A will not see clearly traffic condition from the opposite direction (Fig. 2).

    b.   Driver A will be tempted to go forward to see traffic from the other side (Fig. 3 next page).

Result

    a.   If vehicle A moves forward and can't see traffic clearly from the opposite side, but still turns blindly, collision can happen (Fig. 3).

My defensive techniques in this situation:

    a.   I turn sharply to the left as I move forward to line my vehicle to B (Fig. 4). (See next page.)

    b.   I keep wheels straight while at the middle of the intersection; if turned to the left, I will have an accident, if I'm pushed forward accidentally from the back (Fig. 4).

Note

    a.   Intersections without turning arrows must have the turning lanes in line as much as possible so drivers can see traffic from the other side & not turn blindly (Fig. 5).

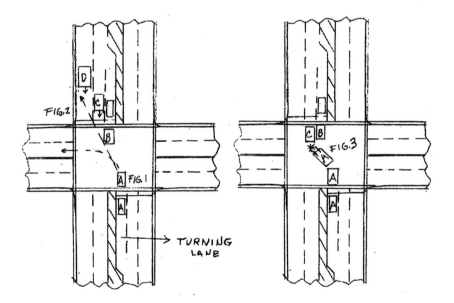

12. Situation 2nd page (fig. 4 and 5).

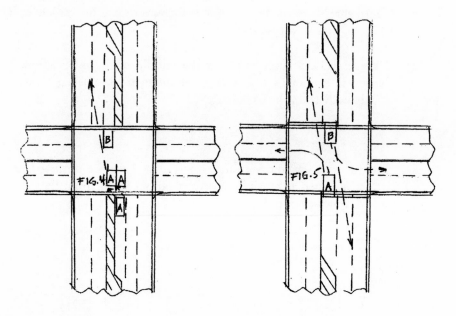

13. Situation

    a.   Vehicle A is driving in the middle lane (Fig. 1 next page).

    b.   Vehicles are allowed to park on the outside lane of the road (Fig. 2).

Danger

    a.   Before crossing the road, some pedestrians don't check for their safety (Fig. 3).

    b.   Drivers that don't check traffic behind before moving forward or opening their door (Fig. 4).

    c.   Passengers using the roadside door to exit without checking traffic behind. (Fig. 5).

    d.   Some drivers also don't take precautions in anticipation of the above dangers.

My defensive techniques in this situation:

    a.   I don't drive next to parked vehicles, except to turn right, to have space cushion (Fig. 6).

    b.   Driving next to parked vehicles, I watch for doors that might open and vehicles with drivers, they might move forward without checking first for safety. (Fig. 4).

    c.   At a distance, for early warning sign, I check for feet under vehicles, a sign of the presence of pedestrians that can cause trouble. (Fig. 7).

Note

    a.   If I have to stop and park by the side of the road, I remind my passengers at the Back to exit using the curb door only. (Fig. 8)

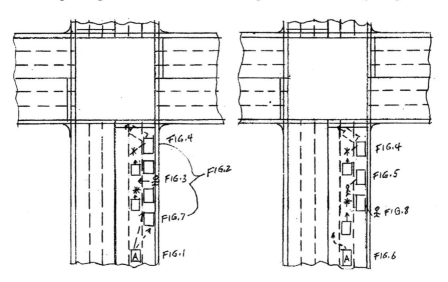

14.   Situation

    a.   Vehicle A is parked at the top of a T intersection (Fig. 1 next page).

Danger

    a.   If somebody is drunk, physically challenged especially at night when cloudy and/or foggy, vehicle A could be broadsided (Fig. 2).

My defensive technique in this situation:

    a.   I park a few feet away from the top of the T intersection to the left or right (Fig. 3).

Note

    a.   I will not contribute to cause accidents have to always consider safety for all.

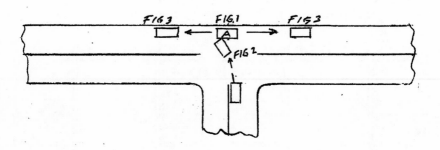

15.   Situation

    a.   Vehicles A, truck or van is parked at the corner entrance of a parking stall (Fig. 1 next page).

Danger

    A.   Due to the size of the truck or van, traffic going in or out from of the parking lot can

        1.   Sideswipe the vehicle (Fig. 2) or

        2.   Limit other driver's view to check for safety (Fig. 3).

My defense in this situation:

a. If I drive bigger than a car, I park anywhere, but not at the corner entrance of a parking stall

Note

a. Drivers should always do things to avoid contributing to an accident.

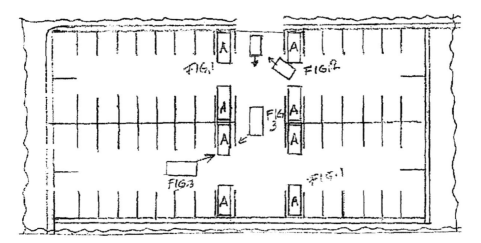

16. Situation

a. Vehicles A just crossed an intersection that is controlled or not, but stops soon after the pedestrian Cross Walk, due to stop and go traffic condition ahead. (Fig. 1 next page)

b. Vehicles B following behind stops before clearing the intersection (Fig. 2).

Danger

a. If any vehicle B can't clear and blocks the intersection, it will cause massive confusion or accident, impede traffic flow, upset drivers to blow their horn. Driver B can be cited and issued a traffic ticket (Fig. 3).

My defensive techniques when traffic is heavy especially at intersections with traffic lights:

a.   When I'm about half a block from the intersection with stale green, I check traffic behind, ease up on my gas pedal, tap and cover my brake in case I have to stop.

b.   I stop before the first crosswalk, and move forward only if I can clear the intersection so as not to block and impede movement of traffic and pedestrians. (Fig. 4).

Note

The qualities of a defensive driver are:

a.   Courteous and a Good Samaritan.

b.   Can see early possible conflict.

c.   Have the knowledge to avoid accidents.

d.   Help regardless of right of way.

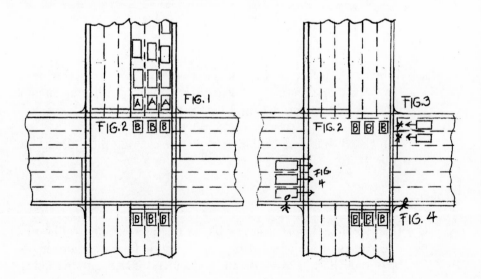

17. Situation

    a. Vehicle A, a van or bigger is parked close to an intersection (Fig. 1).

Danger

    a. It makes it hard for vehicles B and D to check traffic coming from the left side (Fig. 2).

    b. If vehicle B or D moves forward beyond what is safe or proceeds with maneuver although safety not completely verified due to limited view, they could collide with vehicle C. (Fig. 3).

My defensive technique in this situation:

    a. If I'm vehicle B or D, I inch up slowly forward and proceed only when I'm completely sure of my safety and not interfere with oncoming traffic.

Note

    a. Vehicles should not park too close to the intersection, so drivers can check traffic properly.

    b. Drivers should remember that, "a few seconds of caution can save a lifetime of regret."

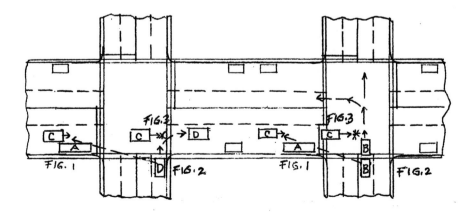

18. Situation

    a.   At an intersections or parking lots, hedges or commercial signs are blocking the view of drivers to check traffic for safety (Fig. 1).

Danger

    a.   Drivers A will not have a good view of traffic conditions (Fig. 1).

    b.   If drivers A are in a hurry to make the turn or go straight, collision can happen (Fig. 2).

My defensive technique in this situation:

    a.   If I'm driver A, I slowly move forward, making sure I don't interfere with pedestrians and/or traffic, knowing that a few seconds of caution is preferable than an accident.

Note

    a.   I report to the government authority, if I see something that can interfere with the Smooth flow of traffic.

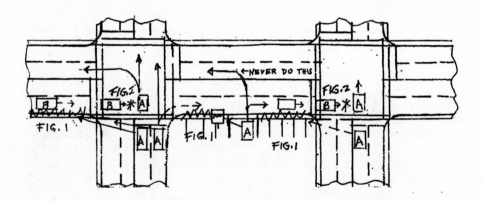

19. Situation

a. Vehicle A, on green light, moves forward to the middle of the intersection for a left turn where there's no turning arrow, and following behind is vehicle B (Fig. 1).

Danger

a. Vehicle B could be stuck or block the intersection and can cause an accident if A can only turn left when the lights turn yellow or red (Fig. 2).

b. Vehicle B could be in collision with traffic from the left (Fig. 2) or from the front (Fig. 3) if B insists to turn left on a red light.

My defensive techniques in this situation:

a. If I'm vehicle B, I will not follow A (Fig. 1 and 2); it's against traffic rules, and I can be stuck or block the intersection causing confusion resulting into an accident.

b. I will only proceed to the intersection, if A has turned and the light is still green.

Note

a. Learn defensive driving and accident avoidance techniques, the road to safety.

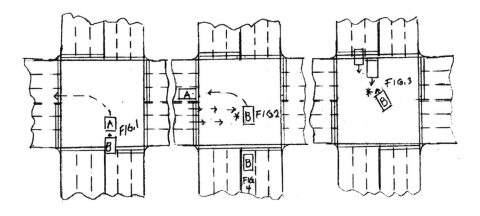

20. Situation

    a.   Vehicle A is turning right at an intersection with red lights (Fig. 1 next page).

    b.   With left turning arrow, vehicle B is turning left from the opposite side (Fig. 2).

Danger

    a.   If vehicle A turns right on red, after stopping if law allows, it can collide with B, who's turning left and wide, if both turn at the same time (Fig. 2).

    b.   Vehicle A can also collide with motorized scooters, cyclists, or pedestrians (Fig. 3, 4, and 5) if A turns right and blind spot is not checked properly.

My defensive techniques in this situation if I'm vehicle A:

    a.   Before I turn right on red, I make sure B is not turning wide to my lane (Fig. 2).

    b.   Also, before I turn right on green, I make sure it's clear of pedestrians, cyclists, and motorized scooters by checking the right outside mirror (Fig. 4) & blind spots (Fig. 5).

Note

    a.   Drivers and pedestrians should check for safety before any maneuver, regardless of who has the right of way? One second may save a lifetime of regret.

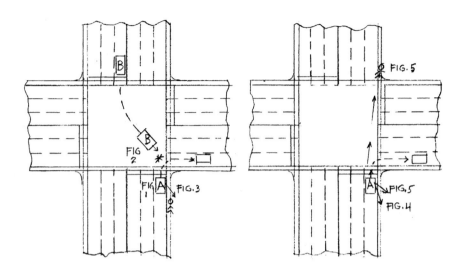

21. Situation

    a.   Vehicle A wants to turn left at an intersection that has no traffic lights. (next page)

Danger

    a.   Vehicle A can collide with pedestrians and/or traffic crossing its path.

My defensive techniques if I'm vehicle A:

    a.   First, as I get close to the intersection, I check for pedestrians and traffic on my left, front, and right side (Fig. 1, 2, 3, 4, and 5) at least twice.

    b.   If clear, I proceed to the middle of the intersection (fig. 8) and still check for pedestrians & traffic (Fig. 6, 7, and 4) as I aim at the lane next to the center lane (Fig. 9).

    c.   I make sure my wheels are not turned to the left and vehicle is not encroaching with the opposite lane, if I have to stop at the intersection (Fig. 8).

Note

    a.   Having no accident yet, should not embolden one to delay learning defensive driving and accident avoidance techniques, sooner or later it will be paid.

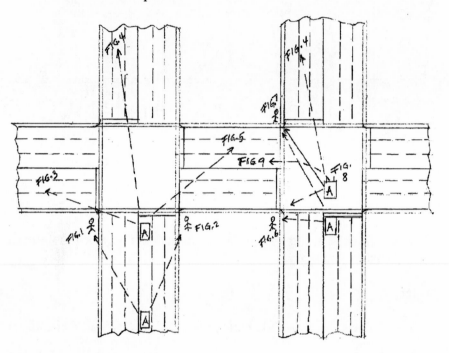

22. Situation

    a.   Due to red lights, vehicle A stops at an intersection (Fig.1 next page, left side).

Danger

    a.   If A moves forward as soon as the green light comes on, without first checking traffic from left and right, can be dangerous. (Fig. 2).

My defense in this situation:

    a.   Knowing that some drivers speed up to cross on yellow or red lights. Before I advance on a green light, I check first traffic from left to right (Fig. 3).

Note

    a.   I never entrust my health or life to others regardless who has the right of way.

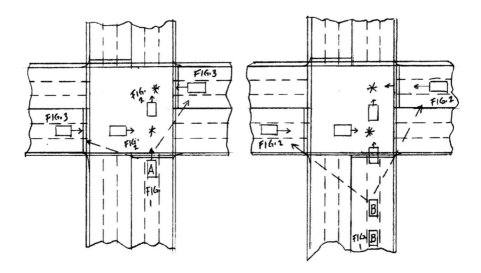

23. Situation

    a.   Vehicle B is approaching an intersection with a green light, giving the right to go through the intersection (Fig. 1 above right side).

Danger

    a.   Even B has green lights; intersection must be checked for traffic crossing its path. (Fig. 2)

My defense in this situation:

    a.   Due to many reasons why drivers don't stop at red lights, before I cross an intersection, regardless whose has the right of way, I check traffic condition first from left to right (Fig. 2) as my health and life are at risk.

Note

    a.   If I'm in a collision that is not even my fault, where will my dream be if tomorrow I'm in an accident?

    b.   It takes only a few seconds to save me, a lifetime of regret.

24. Situation

    a.   After shopping, a driver is backing out from a shopping center's parking lot. (Fig.1 next page)

Danger

    a.   The driver might back up into a vehicle behind, a shopping cart, and/or a pedestrian that doesn't check for their safety.

My defensive techniques in this situation:

    a.   Before entering the vehicle, I check around for presence of obstruction. If available, I ask the help of a passenger to check outside while I back up, especially if I parked beside van or truck. (Fig. 1).

    b.   I take proper backing position and check; straight behind (a), right (b), and left (c). I repeat the steps as needed while backing slowly and stopping frequently. (Fig. 2).

    c.   Preferably, I park at the farthest stall—less vehicles and pedestrians to worry about (Fig. 3).

    d.   It is easier to exit and safer, if I park in front of a vacant stall in tandem (Fig. 4).

    e.   It makes leaving safer and easier if I back up to park (Fig. 5).

    f.   When I back-up, I stop checking behind only, after the maneuver is done.

Note

a. It takes only a few seconds to avoid an accident. Never back up in
a hurry. Practice backing at an empty road or mall, if needed.

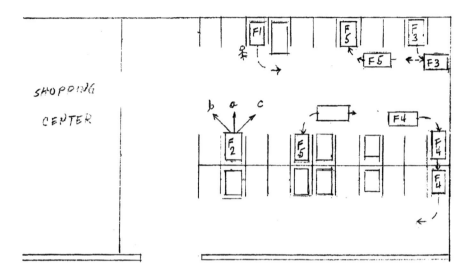

25. Situation

    a.   Driver A is driving between parked vehicles in a busy parking lot. (see next page)

Danger

    a.   Vehicles that are backing either from left or right, if they don't check properly behind, may collide with driver A.

My defensive techniques, if I'm A:

    a.   I drive slowly and defensively while observing parked vehicles from right to left. Not insist on my right of way, to avoid an accident, as I check for the following:

        1.   White backup light (Fig. 1).

        2.   Smoke from tailpipes (Fig. 2).

        3.   Shopping carts parked improperly.

        4.   Vehicle big enough to block the view of the driver to see me (Fig. 3).

        5.   Pedestrians jaywalking and crossing between parked vehicles (Fig. 4).

        6.   Vehicle backing up (fig. 5).

    b.   I tap my horn to warn the driver, if any of the above is observed.

    c.   If backing vehicle ignores warning and keeps backing, I stop for safety.

Note

    a.   If one is knowledgeable on defensive driving and accident avoidance techniques, and one help to avoid an accident, can you imagine how thankful the other driver will be?

b.   I can't see the logic of some drivers who would rather have an accident, than help.

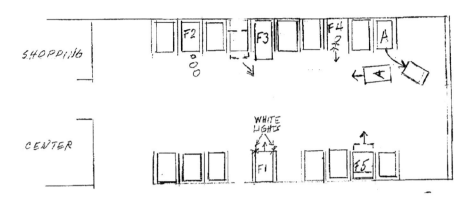

Legend or Meaning of Symbols

1.   *------------Accident or collision.

2.   ![hand] [WAIT]—Stale green, wait or don't walk—green lights about to turn yellow, drivers take precaution.

3.   [walk person] [WALK]—Walk—Green lights are fairly new—Pedestrians can cross, drivers be cautious especially when you're turning.

4.   [bushes] [bushes]—Bushes.

5.   Blind spot—left or right side of vehicle, hides a vehicle/pedestrian from driver's view.

6.   Controlled intersection—has traffic sign, drivers even it's your right of way, still check.

7.   Uncontrolled intersection—must check & speed to conform to traffic, road & weather.

8.   Inside lane—lane next to the yellow line, separating the flow of traffic and for passing.

9. Outside lane—lane next to curb or side walk. Not best lane for driving straight ahead.

10. Middle lane—in between inside & outside lane. Best lane for driving straight through

11. Turning bay—lane for turning left/right. Opposite turning left bays if not inline & without turning arrows, are not very safe. Traffic from the other side can't be viewed.

12. Bus cut off lane—cutoff lane for bus to park when dropping or picking up passengers or while killing time, a must have for safety, not to interfere with the flow of traffic.

Author's Biography

Honesto Marcos has a bachelor's degree in Education, and has been a successful educator in North America and overseas. Was a rehabilitation counselor, an insurance and real estate salesman? He had a very successful driving school business as an owner-operator, driving instructor, critic, and driver examiner. He is held in high esteem in the industry by his colleagues and the numerous safe, successful and grateful former students. A member of Lion's Club, was once voted, "Who is who" by his peers. A member of APDEA, Alberta Professional Driver's Education Association in Canada, composed of driving school owners, driving instructors, driver examiners and Motor Vehicle personnel's involved in driver training and safety.

His whole life has been molded around grateful service to others, ever willing to contribute to a better, safer, happier, productive and more comfortable life to society in general. He believes that no one is a failure until we stop learning. Since vehicle is still the king to commute to work, or shopping that learning defensive driving and accident avoidance techniques even not mandatory but the best solution to prevent traffic accidents.

As a driver for many years, driving instructor and driver examiner, he question why there's too much traffic accidents and ever increasing in spite better roads, vehicles loaded with safety features and driver testing had improved over the years. Also why? drivers that are well mannered elsewhere but become too emotional, hot on the collar and harbor hatred to fellow driver that cause blood pressure to rise.

Honesto knows too well that traffic accidents can result in wasting valuable time, financial resources, and destruction of properties, health and life too is at stake. That most accidents are easy to anticipate thus it is preventable and predictable if only one knows the telltale signs and the defensive technique to abort possible collision.

He has had aver 50 years of extensive driving experience in some of the most pleasurable as well as scary but excellent driving and learning conditions. His Insightful, effective, and practical advice shared in his book is a synthesis of the knowledge, and skills in safe driving he gained extensively as an instructor, examiner and while driving all over North America from the near sub-arctic conditions across the ten provinces of Canada, Spicing up his driving experience, he has also driven through the notorious and challenging traffic congestion of Manila, Philippines, and up and down the long narrow winding roads of the Philippine Cordilleras, where drivers with nary formal driver trainings gleefully dare to "play chicken" with those who are willing.

Taught defensive driving for years, he has always emphasized defensive driving regardless of who have the right of way but has the last clear chance, especially it take only a seconds to avoid a life time of regret. What a joy, he believes; it would be to see happiness to a stranger not expecting help. He believes that it might not completely eliminate all traffic accidents but for sure lessen it. He maintains that:

"Right of way or not, a driver is always ultimately responsible for his own safety and that he share the road environment with. Loss of life, lifelong impairment that impairs health can be financially draining to self and others. Honesto believes that all safety conscious individuals will agree that the only way to avoid traffic conflict is, be well informed on "Defensive Driving and accident Avoidance techniques," to be knowledgeable on how to observe conditions well in advance that can lead to traffic conflict and apply timely the techniques to prevent it.

He recommends that every driver out there be aware that while driving, the world's worst driver could be at any time be coming fast towards you from any direction. Defensive techniques suggested in his book, "1001 Ways to Drive Defensively," are not curve on stone. It's intended to complement and not in any way change or contradict the Driver's manual in your area. But add spice to the defensive techniques and procedures from the department of Motor Vehicles' manual in your state or province. You are protecting one that can't be replaced, even with all the money in the world. Learn defensive driving now, not after an accident. Too late can't be reversed. Honesto advocates that to make driving a happy and accident free experience, as we are all in this crusade, if you have any feedback, personal experience about driving that is educational, memorable, anecdotes and or jokes you can mail to: P.O. Box 73054 Las Vegas, Nevada 89170-3054

CPSIA information can be obtained at www.ICGtesting.com
Printed in the USA
BVOW01s1907190115

383980BV00003B/272/P